8 Weeks to Everlasting

8 Weeks to Everlasting

A Step-by-Step Guide to Getting (and Keeping!) the Guy You Want

AMY LAURENT
Star of Bravo's ***MISS ADVISED***

WITH KRISTEN McGUINESS

St. Martin's Griffin New York

The names and identifying characteristics of some persons described in this book have been changed, as have dates, places, and other details of events depicted in the book.

www.stmartins.com

Design by Patrice Sheridan

LIBRARY OF CONGRESS CATALOGING-IN-PUBLICATION DATA

Laurent, Amy.
8 weeks to everlasting : a step-by-step guide to getting (and keeping!) the guy you want / Amy Laurent with Kristen McGuiness.—1st ed.
p. cm.
ISBN 978-1-250-02062-8 (trade pbk.)
ISBN 978-1-250-02063-5 (e-book)
1. Dating (Social customs) 2. Man-woman relationships. 3. Intimacy (Psychology) I. McGuiness, Kristen. II. Title. III. Title: Eight weeks to everlasting.
HQ801.L328 2012
306.73—dc23 2012016342

ISBN 978-1-250-02062-8

First Edition: August 2012

10 9 8 7 6 5 4 3 2 1

Contents

8 Weeks to Everlasting

Introduction

Dating sucks. You've said it. I've said it. Even your aunt Kathleen has said it. And this is what sucks: walking into a coffee shop, bar, or restaurant, scanning everyone in the room, looking for a man you may have never met, and sitting down for what is basically a job interview with drinks.

Putting yourself out there is challenging no matter the circumstances. Putting yourself out there in the hopes of getting real love and a lasting relationship is like finding yourself in the Olympics after your first swimming lesson—you'll be underwater in no time. But dating can be *wonderful.* Dating the right person can be fun. It can be exciting. And, yes, it can be romantic.

So, let's reframe this.

What do we really mean when we say "dating sucks"?

We mean the first eight weeks.

Think about it. Maybe you have trouble getting past those first few weeks. You act interested, the guy stops calling. You act uninterested, he stops calling. Or maybe you're having trouble even getting past the first date. You bang your head against the wall, wondering, "What is the deal? What am I doing wrong?" So let's try this again. Instead of saying, "Dating sucks," say, "The *initial* stages of dating suck."

Feels better already, doesn't it?

Well, let's not stop there. Because I'm here to tell you that it doesn't need to suck at all. In fact, dating can and should be your new favorite hobby. Instead of viewing it as a necessary evil, start looking at it as fun. Because it can be fun. This could be the chance to meet your next boyfriend . . . or who knows, even your husband. Though I don't think the Cinderella story has done us many favors, the fact is every date you go on is a night at the ball (minus the pumpkin). So get dressed up, put on your favorite music, and allow yourself to feel a little romantic. Even if the first date doesn't go the way you want, it's still a chance to get out of the house and meet someone new. So have fun! Dating can be a powerful, wonderful experience. But first, you have to stop seeing it as a chore, and start seeing it as a way to keep busy and meet new people. And who knows, tonight's date might just be the first step on the road to everlasting.

Dating doesn't have to be like a job interview with drinks. Dating doesn't have to suck.

Here's the thing about dating. Nobody teaches you how to do it. Sure, we sit with our friends and recount our dating horror stories. We answer the magazine quizzes that promise to reveal our "Dating IQ." And we watch those ridiculous romantic comedies, as if Katherine Heigl has anything to teach us—let alone Jennifer Aniston. But nobody really teaches us how to date. Not successfully, anyway.

We go to school to learn how to read and write. We're taught sixteenth-century history and algebra, and we're even shown how to dissect a frog. But nobody, and I mean nobody, shows us how to date. (Although dissecting a frog comes close.) I can promise you, as a single woman I care a lot more today about meeting the right guy and having a successful relationship than I do about knowing who signed the Magna Carta. (Magna *who*?)

You're an intelligent woman. You have interests and goals of your own. And chances are one of those goals is to meet someone you fall in love with. Never mind that "Everlasting Love" has actually been trademarked by a jeweler and a florist, and co-opted by every greeting-card company in the country. You can have real and everlasting love (no trademark!) as long as you're sensible and strategic—as long as you don't buy into the fairy-tale dream made up by marketers. Because creating a real relationship is not a matter of being struck by Cupid's arrow and finding The One. Everlasting love is a goal, and it should be treated like one.

Goals take time, hard work, strategy, and patience. You'd accept that notion, wouldn't you, if your goal was to get a promotion, become certified in yoga, or learn to play the violin? So why should your romantic goals be any different?

They shouldn't be. That's good news, because it means that your goal of finding love is within your reach. Yes, *your* reach. But let me repeat myself here: this goal requires time, hard work, strategy, and patience. Most all of, it requires that you make sound choices . . . particularly in those first eight weeks.

The first eight weeks are the most important part of the dating process. These are the make-it or break-it days (and dates) that separate the couples from the singles. So let's take a step back and evaluate. What are you looking for and where? What do you want in a partner? What do you value, and what do you want to be valued for?

Don't be that fool who's always rushing in. Stop thinking of every first date as The One. Stop making him out to be something he's not, and for heaven's sake, stop making excuses. Most important, stop thinking of the fairy-tale courtship and you may just avoid the fairy-tale divorce. (With apologies to Kim Kardashian.)

The first eight weeks are the make-it or break-it days (and dates) that separate the couples from the singles.

Are you serious about wanting to create a satisfying and lasting relationship? Yes, I said *create,* because you *create* a good relationship—you don't *find* it. If you are, then you need to start applying the same principles that you would to any other worthwhile goal.

Don't know how?

That's where I come in.

I'm a professional matchmaker who has spent the last six years connecting men and women who are too busy to find suitable dates either online or in bars or through their second cousin twice removed. My clients are professional people who are tired of meeting the wrong guy (or the wrong girl), so they come to me in order to find the right one. I have helped hundreds of men and women find love—many of whom have gone on to marry. In fact, I currently have an 80 to 85 percent success rate helping people find a partner within the first three months, and I have been responsible for almost thirty marriages in less than five years. But my job is more than just setting people up; it is helping them after the introductions have been made and the dating begins. Whether it's a guy wondering, "What the heck is she thinking?" or a girl wondering, "What the heck is he thinking?" a major part of my job is to help both parties negotiate those tenuous weeks that can lead to everlasting.

We don't *find* lasting relationships. We *create* them.

I may be a professional matchmaker, but in many ways I'm very much like you. I've dated like you. Acted like you. Cried like you. And over the years, I've bought every dating book on the shelf. I've read about how I'm supposed to be a bitch, how I'm supposed to play the game, how I'm supposed to learn the rules. All of which reinforced my opinion that dating sucks. I'm not sure what it was that sparked the change in me, or when (maybe it was after telling myself one too many times that *he's just not into me*), but I started to pay attention.

I pay attention to what men do and what they say. I pay attention to what women do and what they say. And I pay attention to what men and women do—and say—when they're together. It's all very interesting, I can tell you. But nothing is more interesting than what men say *after* the date has ended.

You think women like to talk about relationships? You've never met my male clients.

I receive e-mails and phone calls almost daily in which my male clients share their thoughts and concerns about the women they date. And it never surprises me that though we all seem to want the same things—a stable career, a loving family, a beautiful life—men and women think very differently about how to go about getting them. From my client Jimmy, who gets annoyed when his date talks negatively about her family or friends ("If she's going to say that about her mother, imagine what she would say about me?"), to Peter, who loses interest if a woman doesn't have any interests of her own ("Amy, every time I ask her what she's doing, she says *nothing,* and asks what I want to do."), I hear it all.

When my clients talk, I listen. Here's your opportunity to listen, too, because they are an incredible source of inside information that we all need to hear. I began reading their feedback and listening to their stories and I started watching what separated the successful relationships from the failed ones. And more often than not, it all came down to one thing: the choices that we women make.

That's right. *We* are the ones who make the choices. *We* are the ones who are in charge.

As the author Milan Kundera once wrote, "Every love relationship is based upon unwritten conventions rashly agreed upon by the lovers during the first weeks of their love. On the one hand, they are living a sort of dream; on the other, they are drawing up the fine print of their contracts like the most hard-nosed of lawyers."

Exactly.

FUN FACT: Women are the ones in charge. We set the tone and, ultimately, we determine what kind of relationship we're going to be in. Hint: It's the one we ask for.

It's entirely up to you whether the contract you're agreeing to is for a relationship filled with fun, friendship, and love, heading to a bright and shiny future . . . or whether you end up dumped, depressed, and obsessed. Or worse, stuck in a relationship with someone you shouldn't be with. Happiness or frustration is a choice you get to make.

And it's all determined in those first eight weeks.

Before You Begin

This book is not about getting the guy. It's about getting the guy you want and not wasting time on the ones who aren't right for you. You have the power to decide who you're in a relationship with—whether it's by your behaviors or by your actual choice.

Most women assume that the opportunity for romance starts on the first date. Well, I'm here to tell you that opportunity begins right now. Yes, *now.* Because there will be no first date until you get some basics down, and that includes the basics of being a woman in the twenty-first century.

You don't need to change a single thing about who you are. But you might need to start changing some of the things you're doing.

Think about it: What separates the daters from the non-daters? It's not beauty or every Hollywood actress would be married. And it's not career or every Hollywood actress would be married. No, it's all about how *you* behave.

Are you a strong, independent woman who has her own hobbies and interests in life? Do you have a network of friends and an active social life whether you're in a relationship or not? Are you out there meeting people, reaching out, being open to going on dates no matter who the person is or what he does for a living? Do you desire a healthy relationship? Or are you just desperate for one?

You don't need to change a single thing about who you are. But you might need to start changing some of the things you're doing.

Because there is nothing that sends a man running like a woman who doesn't want to do anything but obsess over him. That's boring for him, and I promise, you'll get bored pretty quick, too. So let's talk about how to date, and how not to date. It's pretty simple stuff. So simple we all work very hard to complicate it.

This is not about teaching you how to play mind games, or how to pretend you're too cool when you're really a nice, sensitive, and open woman who just wants to say what's on her mind. If that's who you are, own it. But no matter what, you still have to be aware of that little dance everyone does when they're first getting to know someone. You've been messing it up not because you were being yourself, but because you were being yourself while ignoring all the things you need to do in order to build a proper foundation for a relationship.

No more excuses or whining. You need to start dating the right way, the way you were never taught, and yet somehow—miraculously—are supposed to be an expert at.

That's why I'm here.

I am your expert, and it's a role that's been hard won. You see, I've learned these lessons through my own field research. I've been hurt, dumped, and left brokenhearted by men I thought would be my knight in shining armor. And was it always their fault? Sadly, no. Though I have certainly dated my fair share of a**holes, I also had to start looking at myself. What was my part in all this? Where was I to blame? And, like you, I had to learn how to do something different.

Best Foot Forward

Let's face it: first impressions count. I have been on way too many dates were the guy looked as if he just came from the gym. I couldn't help but wonder if he was actually working to *not* impress me. And the same goes for you. Sometimes you may walk into a date looking as if you just rolled out of your bed, or even worse, someone else's bed. In many ways, going on a date is like going on an interview—and for possibly the most important position of your life—so dress like it. This has nothing to do with looks. I am sure if you looked around at all your friends in relationships, you would quickly realize that it's not about being a supermodel.

You need to play the part if you want to get the part.

First impressions are all about the packaging—what you're wearing, how you're carrying yourself, whether you're presenting yourself as a confident and self-assured woman or someone who doesn't have the energy or esteem to put herself together. In order to get the part, you need to play the part. You should wear an outfit that speaks to who you are—this is not about being someone else—an outfit that you'd be comfortable wearing to dinner with your family. No cleavage, no skirts so short you can't bend over, and no heels so high that you can't make it down a flight of stairs. On the other hand, you also don't need to go on the date looking like a nun, so watch out for anything that either hides your body so much he can't see you're a woman or anything too boyish that he mistakes you for one of the guys. As one of my clients recently told me, "There's nothing worse than showing up to a date and she's wearing the same clothes as me." So stay away from power-woman suits or active-wear gym clothes—even if your Lululemon yoga pants look great on you. Basically, if it's nice enough for church or the holidays, then it's nice enough for a date. If you wouldn't wear it in front of a preacher or your grandmother, then don't wear it out with a man you are meeting for the first time.

The same goes with your grooming. If you usually don't do your hair or wear makeup, fine. But you can manage to pull out the hairbrush and put on some Chapstick so you look fresh in your natural beauty. You want him to see that this date is important to you. You don't need to look like you're about to step onto the red carpet, but you do need to get ready with the intention that you might be meeting someone very important. You would want him to look nice for you, so how about looking nice for him?

STAY TRUE TO YOURSELF

When it comes to dating, you should never be someone you're not. For example, I can't stop talking. Ever. I've been this way since I was a little kid and you're certainly not going to get me to stop now. Especially not for a man. When I go on dates, I am the same silly, bubbly, energetic nonstop talker that I am in every situation in my life. I wish I could come in and be some mysterious Angelina Jolie type, all brooding and sexy, but I can't.

But that's not a problem. I know from the men I have dated that they love my energy. I make them laugh and feel at ease, and they have a lot of fun in my presence. The problem is not my personality. Nor is it yours. You are fine just as you are. Whether you're an extrovert like me or the quiet and mysterious type like Ms. Jolie, the trouble doesn't come in who you are, but rather in how you act.

The Power of Positive Dating

For any woman who complains that there aren't any good men out there, my first question is: Are you looking for them? Because I'll tell you right now, Mr. Right is not circling your block, waiting for you to come out of your house. And if there is someone doing that, call the cops. Now.

Mr. Right is out busy living his life. He's sitting in traffic listening to morning radio. He's answering his phone at the office and rolling his eyes at his boss. He's out with his friends, playing darts at the corner bar, and scoping the room for a cute girl. He's going back to his apartment at night and watching *Sports Center* while he checks his e-mails before he goes to bed. He is busy. But he is also waiting for you.

And here is your chance to find him.

But first you need to leave the house.

If you're going to be a powerful dater, you need to have a powerful life. You, like him, need to be busy. Because one of the things I do remember from years in school learning stuff I can no longer apply is that a body in motion stays in motion. The same goes with dating. If you are out there, having a good time, you will attract people who are looking to have a good time with you.

If you're going to be a powerful dater, you need to have a powerful life.

WHERE THE BOYS ARE

There are men everywhere. I mean that. Go over to your local market right now to pick up some milk, and chances are you will see one. They are out there and they're actually easy to meet. You just need to ask the right people and get out to the right places. Here are eight suggestions.

1. **Bars and restaurants.** I know people say you'll never meet your boyfriend at a bar but that is *so* not true. As long you only give him your number, and don't go home with him, your future boyfriend could be at your corner pub or restaurant right now.
2. **Friends and family.** Let's face it. They know people. A lot of people. Some of whom are probably wonderful single men. Don't be afraid to send an e-mail or make some phone calls and ask for their help.
3. **The office.** Workplace romance? This can be a little difficult to negotiate. However, we spend most of our time at the office, so don't shut someone down just because you work with him. And don't be afraid to ask your coworkers if they have any single friends.

4. **Online dating.** By far the easiest way to get a date these days. Sure, there might be a lot of frogs on the Internet sites, but there are also a lot of princes. Match, eHarmony, OKCupid all have eligible men looking for eligible women.
5. **Intramural sports.** Though it's important you maintain your role as the girl in a relationship, let's face it, most guys love sports. So if there is a sport you love, find a coed IM team and join it.
6. **Hobbies.** Remember when you were a kid and you played piano or took a pottery class? Well, it's time to find that inner child and take classes in things that you've always wanted to do, especially ones with other people—no private lessons. You'd be surprised how many men are doing the same thing, and how many cute teachers are leading them.
7. **Concerts, comedy clubs, sporting events.** Basically any public place where people gather—you're not going to find a guy in your living room, so go where the people are. Get tickets to your town's basketball team, hit the movies with some friends, and see your favorite band play. If you're willing to flirt, you can meet a guy anywhere.

8. **Community events.** From the farmers' market to street fairs to volunteer events, your future boyfriend could be right around the corner from you. Check out your community calendar and get out there.

Be the change you wish to see. Stop making excuses that keep you in the dating closet. Sit down and list what stops you from dating. Put it all down—the fears, the challenges, the excuses. And then start seeing what you can change and what you can't. Get into action on what you can. None of us is perfect. Even Halle Berry has bad days. (Perhaps.) Start now to put into action what you need to do in order to feel good about yourself and your life.

Join a gym. Work on some self-love. Look for the job that's right for you. Then let go of the rest. This is not an overnight process but it also doesn't need to take over your life. If you start taking some simple steps now, you will build your confidence and your self-worth. And you will quickly become a powerful dater, not to mention a pretty busy (and happy!) woman.

You Can't Get What You Want If You Don't Know What You Want

It's important to have a clear and concise roadmap to meeting and getting the one you want. Yes, the one *you* want.

Falling in love isn't just a matter of fate, it's a matter of you going out and making the right choices and creating the right environment for love to grow.

Because here's the thing: What almost all men realize, and yet oddly, what most women forget, is that you are the one in control. Yes, you, lady! No matter how long you date, or whether things end up working out or not, you are the one who holds the power. Unfortunately, most of us are not aware of this important fact, so we end up feeling completely out of control, giving away our most important tool to successful dating.

The first step to taking back control is to figure out what you're looking for in the first place. I know way too many women who start dating a man, and halfway through the first few weeks, somehow decide that they were looking for someone entirely different. Don't forget that you get to choose who you're with. This is your adventure, so don't let just anyone join you on it.

Years ago, a friend told me to write down the top qualities I was looking for in a guy. It could include looks, but really the most important things were about who he was on the inside.

This is my list:

1. Funny
2. Kind
3. Loves his job
4. Wants a family
5. Tall (sorry, but I love tall guys)
6. Loyal
7. Smart
8. Knows how to treat a lady

I have since used that list as a guide. Whenever I start dating someone, I pull it out and see if he fits the criteria.

Now, do I break up with him just because one thing is off? No way. But I also keep my priorities in mind, making sure that I am getting into a relationship that honors what's on my list—most of the time. Look, we aren't perfect, and certainly, I'm not. But I can promise you that if you are willing to do the work that it takes to date, you will get better at it, and you will start having fun.

What does your list look like?

Trust the Process

The next guy you go on a date with might be the love of your life, but chances are you're going to have to kiss (and I mean only kiss) a few more frogs before you get to the prince. (No dissecting, please.) I hope that for every date, you refer to this book and think about—really think about—what your approach is going to be for those first eight weeks. This isn't a novel that you read once and toss on your bookshelf. This is a living reference that you should be highlighting, underlining, bookmarking, and picking up every time you need a little friendly advice. It's just like the relationship I have with my clients who call or e-mail whenever they have a dating question or problem. But lucky you—you have all the same answers in this book.

I'm not saying it's going to be easy, and I am not saying that all of these guidelines will feel natural at first. But if you put in the effort, you will realize the power you've had all along: the power to find everlasting love in this otherwise crazy world.

Are you up for it?

Week One

Date Like *This*, Not Like *That*

What Am I Doing Wrong?

It all starts with that very first date. You could have the best third date on the planet (think of blushing from his sweet compliments, laughing so hard you actually snort). You could be having dinner with him in Week Six when it dawns on you that the guy sitting across the table might just turn out to be a very important person in your life. And you could enter Week Eight with a new boyfriend who has met your friends and is eager to meet your family. But none of that is going to happen if you don't make it past that first date.

That's the good news.

And that's the bad news.

It's good news because who doesn't like a fresh start and a new opportunity? It's bad news, because, well, the first date is one of those things that's easy to screw up. Far too easy.

Just recently, for example, I was sitting at my desk on a cloudy Monday morning, hammering away at the keys of my computer, when the first call came in.

"Amy," I heard my client Leslie squeak. I could tell she had been crying and hoped that it wasn't about her date with Paul. This was Leslie's second match-up with me. Unfortunately, she didn't make it very far with the first guy, Jim. To hear Leslie tell it, that first date with Jim went well enough: They had dinner at a Moroccan restaurant and laughed as a belly dancer came to their table. Jim had an adventurous streak, and being a world traveler herself, Leslie liked that in a man. But things traveled too far, too fast, and Leslie later admitted to going back up to Jim's apartment to "play Scrabble." Leslie didn't tell me what happened. She didn't need to. This wasn't about triple word scores or who could get rid of the "q," so whether or not they actually played Scrabble was beside the point. A few days later, when Leslie hadn't heard from Jim, she called him and asked him out. Oh, Leslie! Jim agreed, and this time—Scrabble schmabble—she didn't even bother to give an excuse about why they went back to his place. She called me the next day, and shared, as though it was no big deal, "We had great sex!"

Every first date offers a fresh start and a new opportunity.

Jim never contacted Leslie again, but he did call me to tell me that she wasn't his type. That was it. She "just wasn't his type." Leslie (who by Jim's own account was undeniably beautiful, successful, and funny) asked what type Jim might have been looking for.

"The kind who doesn't go back to his apartment after the first date and the kind that doesn't have sex on date two," I replied.

So I braced myself to hear why Leslie was crying. I hoped she hadn't made the same mistake again. "I didn't," she practically shrieked. "Paul and I just had dinner. It went really great! Outside the restaurant, we had a quick peck and I left in my own taxi. But he's been silent the past few days. He told me how he loved the Jets so I texted him yesterday to say how great it is that they won, and he didn't even text back."

I could hear her getting upset again as she finally unleashed the question I hear from women every day: "What am I doing wrong?"

A lot. But we can all stop that now if we start dating like *this* and stop dating like *that.*

Learning the Right Way to Date

Going back to a guy's apartment on the first date. Sleeping with him on the second. Sending a text after not hearing back for a few days. These were all mistakes Leslie made and they come under the heading of *not building a solid foundation.* We've all acted like Leslie at one time or another. We think it's romantic to wing it or that having a strategy is manipulative. Think again. Remember that first-date analogy: a job interview with drinks? Well, you wouldn't go on an interview and take a job as an accountant if you're really a lawyer, would you? So why settle for something that's unlikely to go any further than the first few dates when what you really want is a long-lasting relationship?

You don't have to settle.

But you do have to build the foundation.

The first date is probably one of the most important meetings the two of you will ever have. But guess what? It's not your job to make it happen. You see, it's the man who should be taking the initiative here—setting the date, choosing the meeting place, and making it a special night for you both, even if it's just drinks or coffee.

If he cares enough about you to give you the right kind of care and attention on the first date, chances are it will continue through subsequent dates. That's right—to a certain extent, how you and he behave on this first date will be reflected in your second. And your third. And your fourth. Sense a pattern? The first week is all about setting the foundation for the weeks to come.

---

influence *n.*: 1. The power of a person to produce an effect upon another, often indirectly. 2. Your ability to make your needs a priority by barely saying a word. 3. The control you exert over your date, without him even knowing it.

There is a difference between *initiative* and *influence.* He may take the initiative in asking you out, setting things up,

> For most of the major decisions in the first eight weeks (outside of sex), you should let him initiate. This isn't because he's a man and has a testosterone-driven need to do so (although that's part of it). This is so that you can see that he's willing to do the work.

and otherwise organizing your date, but it's up to you to oh-so-subtly exert your influence so that he will consider and respect you in the process.

So, while he might be the one making the plans, you are the one who gets to agree to them or not. He asks you out; it's up to you to say yes. He asks when; it's up to you to pick the schedule. He asks where; it's up you to pick the neighborhood.

Think you're being passive? Think again. You have the power of veto here, and that's about as close to a superpower as you can get. So use your powers for good. Use your powers for you! Never be the one to initiate. Do not send the first text. Do not make the first phone call. And do not ask him out. Ever.

Date Like *This*: Plan Ahead

He is asking you out on a first date because he wants to get to know you. And when a man meets a woman he really wants to know, he wants to show off. He will make it a special evening, take you to a place he loves or that speaks to who he is. He will take the time to think when and where would be best—and he will want to make it easy for you to say yes.

When a man meets a woman he really wants to know, he will want to show off. Let him.

One of my favorite female clients is a consultant for a software company. Jennifer spends most of her day making all the decisions, but when it comes to dating, she wants a man who knows how to take charge. Because there's the great irony—though we are the ones in charge, it's important that we are with men who know how to do the same. Unfortunately, Jen's attempts to meet up with my client Doug not only made her feel like the man, they made her feel pretty unwanted, too. Not the way you want to start a date.

From: Jennifer
Subject: Doug

Hey Amy,
So I know you've been wondering about Doug, the real-estate guy . . . unfortunately I don't think I will meet him. After we tried to make both our schedules work for the last few months, he was nice enough to ask me to pick the dinner spot—which I did. We were supposed to have dinner tonight. However, he didn't make the reservation and my assistant had to do it (she called to check). So I'm a bit turned off and I don't think I want to meet him. I'm

sure he's a nice guy, but chivalry is very important to me. He could have just forgotten but I actually think he left it up to me since I picked the restaurant. I don't mean to be picky but generally how a guy behaves so early on is a good indication of how he will be later on.

Next!
Jenny

Not Like *That*: The Casual

Never go out with a guy who won't make the arrangements, and never go out with a guy the same day he asks you out. Let me repeat that: Never go out with a guy the same day he asks you out. You are not some casual he calls on the same day, asking, "Hey, what are you doing later? Wanna grab a beer?" That's not planning ahead. That's not even a date. Remember, you define boundaries when you say no to same-day dates, and yes, this means even when you're really bored and have nothing else to do. Tell him you are busy but that you have the next night free, and he'll quickly learn that if he wants to see you, he needs to actually *make* plans with you.

Asking someone out for the same night is like showing up at the movie theater and buying a ticket to whatever is playing next. You may get to see a romantic comedy or you may see a horror flick. What do *you* want to see?

Date Like *This*: Raise Your Voice

Your voice is the most powerful and important communication tool you own. Use it. You may be an incredibly busy person who uses text and e-mail for work, but this is not work. Besides, you can't build a relationship through e-mail. Talking on the phone is an important part of getting to know someone and an important first step to developing one of the most important and intimate relationships of your life. Once you are in the relationship, you're not going to rely on communicating through text and e-mail (unless for scheduling or for convenience). No, you're going to meet face-to-face and talk. Start practicing that now. If you are able to get comfortable on the phone, it will only help to decrease those first-date nerves, making even the blindest date feel less blind.

Not Like *That*: The Texting Trap

If you start as a text girl, you will always be a text girl. He will not call you to say how wonderful you are, and what a great time he had . . . he will text you. Don't let this happen. If he texts you before the date, stop him. Say that you would prefer that he call. Give him a good time and the best number, so that you can reach each other and not get caught in missed-call hell. Here is the difference between initiative and influence. He is initiating but you're influencing how that initiation takes place. Too many people use texting as an easy and convenient way to communicate and you should be neither easy nor convenient. By influencing him away from making you just another text in his world, you start setting yourself up as a special woman in his life who should be called and spoken with, not texted to.

Now, this doesn't mean you never text! Like all things, there is a time and place for handheld messaging, such as if you are running late or he is sending you the restaurant's information. There are times when you need convenient communication. But leave it at that. Getting to know each other should not be convenient; it should be personal.

Date Like *This*: I Have Something You Don't Have

Women are a freaking miracle. We are amazing, powerful beings. And we have something men don't have. Yes, my friend, you are your own personal jewel of the Nile. And believe you me, if you treat yourself that way, so will any half-decent man who comes into contact with you.

FUN FACT: You are not a boy. I don't care how much football you watch, or how many mountains you have hiked. I don't care that you run your own company, or have an alphabet of degrees after your name. If you look down right now, you will quickly realize that you have girl parts. Very important girl parts.

That's why you need to not only believe it for yourself, but also act that way with him. This goes from the things we say to the things we do: no excessive drinking (and by this, I mean no more than two drinks and *no martinis,* which are the quickest way to an accidental drunk), no dirty humor, and no pretending that you are his frat brother. If you remember back to Leslie, my client who sent the text about the Jets after her first date, you will quickly see why being a lady is one of the most important qualities you have, so don't shed it too soon. That doesn't mean that you can't spend years tailgating with your man and playing fantasy football with the best of them, but don't start that way. That is not your best foot forward. That is your football cleat forward. You need to lead with your most romantic, female side. Because though you might not be comfortable in the glass slipper, it reminds Prince Charming that you are a princess, worthy of his devotion, his time, and his undivided attention. So, remember, glass slipper. Ditch the cleat.

Not Like *That*: One of the Guys

I have a good guy friend Stephen who I tell everything. We have beers like two bros hanging out at the bar. We go to baseball games together. But I'm not trying to date Stephen. In fact, the thought horrifies both of us. Stephen and I act like siblings. But you don't want to become sisterized with someone you feel romantic about.

You've all heard it. The guy that describes his gal pal as "She's like a sister to me." And guys—at least the right kind—do not want to marry their sisters. Their sisters are the women they got into wrestling matches with, the women they like to burp and fart around just to make them mad. Their sisters have probably seen them hock a loogie just to see how high in the air they could spit it.

You do not want to be his sister.

Take Your Time

Recently, I was at brunch with friends when we started talking about some recent first dates we've had. One of my friends Danielle told us about a first and only date she had with a high school teacher whom she really liked. Danielle is short, and more on the cherubic chubby side, but when it comes to men, she is one of the most popular women I know. Guys love her. Unfortunately Danielle has had trouble finding one she loves back. Until she met Jacob online. She explained, "He was so funny, and in the right way, you know. Not mean funny, sweet funny. We had so much fun talking on the phone, and I felt like we were on our first date forever. We shared everything about our lives. I thought for sure I had met The One. But then he never called me again."

If you move slowly, the relationship will move slowly. Take your time. And don't rush it . . . any of it.

I could have predicted that when she said, "We shared everything about our lives." Why would a man want to go out with you again when it seems like he spent a lifetime with you in one night? This is the appetizer, not the main course. Your goal is to whet his palate for more without offering him the whole smorgasbord the first night.

Date Like *This*: Keep It Light

Keep the conversation light and fun. If it sounds like something you would only tell a friend you've known for a while, or if it digs too deep or is something you have at one point cried over, don't bring it up. That doesn't mean you have to dumb it down—but imagine that the date is an episode of *Modern Family,* not a Lifetime movie. You can talk about work and travel and the good parts about your family and childhood. You can talk about food and the city you live in and the fun things you do when you're not going on dates.

Before you go out on the date, think about what you would want to share with him. And think about the questions and topics about which you want to ask him. They should run along these lines:

- What do you do when you're *not* at work?
- Where have you traveled? Where would you like to go?
- Family and light stories of what it was like growing up.

- Anecdotes about the city in which you both live.
- Sports or other shared hobbies or passions.

The conversation should stay positive. It should be funny and light. You should be laughing at least 30 percent of the time. And neither of you have to be a comedian to make that happen, because when a man and woman connect, both smile and laugh. You should be enjoying yourself, not sharing everything about your life.

Not Like *That*: TMI

Unfortunately, many women look at a date as a once-in-a-lifetime chance to show a man everything they have to offer, including the bad stuff. If you fear that you will never see him again, then telling him about your alcoholic mother is not going to help your chances. And yes, of course, you ultimately want to be in a relationship with someone who accepts you and supports you through all the good and bad stuff, but is that a test he needs to pass on the first date? No.

If you act like this is your only chance to make an impression on your date, you're sure to wind up giving him too much information. You know—TMI. And what qualifies as too much information these days? A lot of people don't know. So much of who we are is out there on the Internet that we forget some cards are best not shown up front. Here are the topics that should be left at home on the first date:

- Ex-boyfriends, ex-girlfriends, past romantic or sexual partners of any kind
- Any medical, health, or emotional problems
- Politics, religion, race, and anything that can be voted on
- Family secrets of any kind
- Complaints—he doesn't need to know what's going wrong in your life.

Date Like *This*: Accentuate the Positive

First of all, dating should be fun. You should be having a good time, and you should make sure your guy knows this. Whenever I'm on a date, whether I like the guy or not, I make sure to laugh at all of his jokes. It doesn't matter if they were less funny than sitting through a Rob Schneider movie, I crack up anyway. And you know what happens then? He starts laughing, and even if the date is a bust, we both end up having a lot more fun. Because it's a proven fact that laugh-

> Just because you feel like you have "known him forever" doesn't mean you should act like you have. Leave out the fact that your brother is in jail or that your parent's divorce ruined your life. And for goodness' sake, now is not the time to discuss your prescriptions, diagnoses, therapeutic issues, and lactose intolerance.

ter, and the chemicals released by it, makes you happy. Even if things aren't going well.

Dates are loaded with pitfalls—bad food, terrible service, a nervous and stuttering date—but none of it is made better by being cold or a snob. So go in there with your best "Pollyanna positive" attitude. Make light of a ditzy waitress, and when the food is bad, laugh and shrug it off, saying, "It's better than my mom's cooking." You're there to have a good time no matter what the circumstances. Because dating will be a heck of a lot easier and enjoyable if you stay positive. Moreover, it will help pave the way for a second date—if that's something you want.

Not Like *This*: The Complaint Department

Far too many times I've seen what happens when women come to the dating table with a fistful of complaints. "The food here is terrible" is the same thing as saying "I would rather be at home eating by myself." Likewise, if you don't like your job, now is not the time to go into detail about your lousy boss and that missed promotion. You want to lead with your best foot forward, right? And if you don't believe me, just listen to one of my clients who went out with a woman who had been in the dating closet for years. Melissa hated her job, hated her ex-boyfriends, and apparently, hated any food that wasn't eaten in the comfort of her own home. Would you want to go out with Melissa? Peter certainly didn't.

From: Peter
Subject: Melissa Feedback Form

Amy,
That was one of the worst dates I think I've ever had. Melissa showed up to the restaurant and complained about how loud it was before we even started speaking. She sent her food back three times and then kept talking about how she gets migraines and runs low on energy at night. I couldn't wait for dinner to be over. Afterward, it took a while to get a cab so I stayed with her for twenty minutes. At one point, she thought she had one but there was actually an elderly couple in front of us that took it first because they were there. She cursed them out so loudly I couldn't believe it. It was no surprise I was her first date in a while.

Peter

A Kiss Is Just a Kiss—Really?

So you've made it through the big first night. You've spoken with him on the phone, set up a convenient place to meet, and allowed him to set and plan the date. You've had your dinner, drinks, or coffee, and the conversation was comfortable and fun. You laughed a lot, and stayed away from anything negative. He's now walked you to your car, or a cab, or the bus, and he says that he wants to see you again. You say yes not because you have to, but because you want to. And if you don't want to, tell him you'll think about it, and do that. Go home and ask yourself, "What would it hurt to see him again?"

Sometimes the first date isn't the best. People get nervous; they're not always sure what to do and what to say. You would want a guy to give you the benefit of the doubt so why not offer the same to him?

Let's say you've decided to go out again and he leans in for the kiss. What do you do? Well, first, do you want to kiss him? If you're not sure, this is one of the first physical boundaries you need to set. There is an infinite amount of distance between the friendly peck and the full-on make-out, and you get to set the stage. Right here, right now.

I have been on plenty of dates where we both had a great time and we were feeling the chemistry, but we were also still getting to know each other. A kiss would have felt awkward or forced, so rather than doing something we were unsure about, it felt better to wait. Don't underestimate the hug. It can hold back the kiss for another date and still give you an opportunity to show that you're interested.

Date Like *This*: The Modest Kiss

But if you are going to kiss, the best kiss you can give is the same one you would give at the altar: sweet, engaged, but also modest. Unless you're one of those people who plan to make out in front of your eighty-nine-year-old grandfather on your wedding day, most people know this kiss from every wedding scene in Hollywood history. And what does that look like? Closed mouth, yet open lipped, something that shows him that you are not a cold fish, that you are interested, but that you don't need to mix tongues to get the point across.

Obviously not every kiss is going to go just like that, but the main point to keep in mind is that you don't need to play three-minute tonsil hockey after the first date. By keeping it modest, he will walk away with visions of you in his head. And without even having to say it, you have practiced a kiss ready for wedding bells, not the beginning of a one-night stand.

Sex is easy. It's relationships that are hard.

Not Like *That*: First-Date Sex

So let's talk about the one-night stand. I always tell my clients, "If you don't want a relationship then do whatever you want on a first date." Have a romp for one night, feel free to take him home, but don't plan on calling him your boyfriend anytime soon.

If you do want a relationship, then it's simple: no sex on the first date. Ever. In fact, no sex until you are in an exclusive relationship, but we will discuss that farther down the road. We have all seen or had it happen far too many times.

We meet a great guy. We like him; he likes us. We think it's headed in the right direction, and so we think, "Oh, heck, why not?" I'll tell you why not. Because a guy has to bond emotionally before he has sex, or he won't be interested in bonding at all. For us women, we emotionally bond *when* we have sex. So what happens after a one-night stand? The guy is ready to move on, and you are ready to move in. And, yes, I know a lot of us have had sex for fun, but if you really want a relationship, how about having sex for love?

---

friends with benefits *n.*: two friends who have a sexual relationship without being emotionally involved; a wasteful distraction that will cause you to put your energy into a relationship that, by definition, is going nowhere.

Sadly, more often than not, that guy who was so great, who was so into you, quickly disappears when copulation comes before commitment. As Nigel, one of my most commitment-loving clients, explains, when a woman sleeps with him on the first date, it makes him question the woman:

From: Nigel
Subject: Last night

Hi Amy,
Can't think of any way to give you details without sounding mean. Angie's a very nice person and has a huge heart, but we are just not a good fit. We do not

CHECK PLEASE

Besides "What did I do wrong?" one of the other questions I am most often asked is "Should I offer to pay?" And here's the easy answer: no. Now, does that mean you should be rude? Also, no. Some men may love bitches, but most men just love a lady with manners. This is why the most important words you can say are "Thank you."

If a man has asked you out, he should also be the one to pay. Sure, down the road, when you are heading out to dinner three to four times a week with brunch on the weekend, halfsies makes sense, but not until then. Don't offer, and don't reach for your wallet. It's awkward and it says that you don't think you are deserving of a four-dollar coffee or even a forty-dollar entree. You are, and if you don't believe that, neither will he.

But that also means you shouldn't take his generosity for granted. Make a gesture, put your hand on his, or lean across the table, and say, quite clearly, "Thank you for dinner/coffee/drinks." That's all. "Thank you." Two simple words that tell him who you are.

connect intellectually. She's demonstrated a propensity for making bad decisions. Having sex on the first date did not help. I know it takes two to tango and all that, but c'mon. What was I supposed to do? Say no? And then she called me today, which was just awkward. Please do not tell Angie any of this. I don't want to hurt her feelings.

N.

Now, I'm not saying it was entirely Angie's fault, but let's assume nine times out of ten, a guy will always say yes to sex on a first date. Stay in control of the situation by saying no.

Date Like *This*: Miss Play It Cool

Recently, one of my clients wrote to me explaining that the one thing he liked most about certain women was a quality he didn't know how to name. For some of us, we might just say it's a little je ne sais quoi. But as a journalist, Jeremy tried to do his best to pin it down. He finally started dating again after a bad breakup last year, and what he found was a lot of hungry women. He explained:

From: Jeremy
Subject: The Ladies

Wow—I guess being with one person for ten years had its perks. It's hard out there. I feel like every date I go on, the woman is eyeing me to see whether I would make a good husband. I can tell you, it's not attractive in the least. What is attractive? A woman who is interested in me but doesn't rub my face in it. A woman who has her own thing going on, and her own life, and who is excited to meet me, but clearly can survive if things don't go well. A woman who walks into a room, and it doesn't matter whether she is the prettiest one, but she acts like it. Don't get me wrong—I know there are a lot of women like this out there—but I feel like I keep meeting women who are spending their time waiting for the right guy. For me, that is the wrong girl.

J.

Don't be the wrong girl. Be the one who walks into the room thinking she is the prettiest one there, and who can show interest without making it the next day's front-page news. Stay cool and show him that you might have had a good time but you'll probably be on to the next date unless he makes a strong and good impression. Remember, you might be on a job interview, but ultimately, you are the one in charge of the hiring. So act like it. Sit back and allow him to impress you. And when the date is over, allow him to remind you that he exists. And if he doesn't want the job, then get on your next date and find someone who does.

Not Like *That*: Miss Desperate

It's the next day, or worse, three days later. You haven't heard from him. No calls, no e-mails, not even a text. What does this mean? It means don't waste your time. This is why you need to create a busy life. Because if you have enough going on—whether it's work or hobbies or other dates—then you will value your time, not wanting to waste another breath on someone who isn't into you. You can use the week to see what you've done right, what mistakes you might have made, and what you will do differently next time. Whatever you do, don't react out of fear. I've seen too many women panic, believing that their whole self-worth comes down to whether a guy likes them or not.

There is no bigger turn-off, and no bigger act of desperation, than to be the one to follow up. You thank him that night and then you give him forty-eight hours to get back in touch, and if he doesn't, then you start getting ready for the next guy. And how do you find him? I know that most of us do not have men lined up around the corner waiting for us, and chances are you do not have a professional matchmaker like me working on your behalf. But you do have some pretty powerful resources: the Internet, friends, family members, the gym, hobbies, work—all places and people who can matchmake for you. So ask your cousin if he has any single friends, take your headphones out of your ears at the gym, and start going for coffee or even to a casual bar alone. It is much easier to be picked up when you're not engrossed in conversation with your best friends.

He hasn't called since your first date? Move on. You do not need to pine over someone with whom you spent only three hours on a Thursday evening. You spend more time with your hairdresser.

And if you haven't already, get on the Internet now. There are a lot of wonderful dating sites with scores of eligible men who are interested in meeting the right person. They're not on there just to have sex or waste your time. They want a relationship and are willing to create a profile and go on some blind dates in order to get it. So why can't you?

Not everyone is going to be for everyone and if this guy isn't right, start looking for someone else, and stop obsessing about the one who hasn't called. I know that's hard. I have sat by my phone waiting for the text or call way too many nights, hoping that every time I hear a ring, it's him on the other line. I know what a horrible waste of time and energy it is, and I've learned my lesson.

I have one client who wouldn't waste three hours mourning a failed business deal. Maria runs her own executive consulting company, helping top CEOs locate available executive staff, and in her line of work, she is used to rejection. Maria is smart and beautiful; all the CEOs love working with her. But they don't always take her clients. She shares, "They'll let me know that they found someone else, or they didn't like my pick. I don't think about it for more than thirty minutes. I'll look at the candidate and see where I failed to pick the right match, or what I could have done differently. I find the lesson in it, and move on. But if it's a date, forget it. It's like I have a trigger finger."

I have Maria on a next-day watch. Every time she wants to call or text the guy in question, she calls or texts me. And I suggest the same for you—create a buddy system. Call a friend every time you are tempted to call him, and see how you can begin to relinquish the obsession. At first, my phone was blowing up the day after one of Maria's dates, but now she's getting used to it. She tells me, "If I've been out with someone who doesn't want to or doesn't know how to connect afterward, then I've realized that I'm wasting my time, and his, to try to follow up. I'm trying to do the same thing after my dates that I do at work. I give myself thirty minutes to figure out what I could have done differently, then I move on."

WEEK ONE: CHOOSE YOUR OWN RELATIONSHIP

This book is not about getting just any guy. It's about getting the guy you want and not wasting time on ones who aren't right for you. You have the power to decide who to pursue a relationship with. When I was a kid, I loved those choose-your-own-adventure books. It felt like any story could end up exactly as I wanted. And I don't think relationships are so different. If you meet a guy you want to date, and you follow the steps to secure yourself the next date, and the next, and the next, chances are you will find yourself in the relationship you have always wanted. But if you are seeing someone who isn't treating you with the respect, kindness, and the affection he should, then you'll now be able to cut the guy loose without going through the anxiety and disappointment we women typically experience when dating. Every minute you spend with the wrong guy is a minute you could be spending finding the right one.

Believe that you deserve a relationship where you are treated like a lady, and where you never have to wonder whether he is into you or not. Leave him wanting more, and he will. I can't guarantee that if you take all these steps in the first week that you will be together forever, but I can promise that if you want to, you will find yourself heading into the next phase of your relationship: Week Two.

Eight Steps to Everlasting

1. Do not be the one to initiate.
2. Do not go out the same day he asks.
3. Do not send the first text.
4. Do not act like his buddy.
5. Do not make the first phone call.
6. Do not have sex.
7. Do not ask him out. Ever.
8. Do have fun!

Week Two

Getting to Know Him

Why Do I Need to Stop Crushing?

Date one went well and now you've had date two . . . or maybe even date three. He's initiating, planning in advance, and in general, acting interested. And the feeling is mutual. You can't wait for the next date. You think about him during work, and anticipate that little beep on your phone alerting you to a missed call. You're crushing hard. And you need to stop yourself right now.

The minute we find someone attractive, it's like we lose our minds. Chemicals flood our brains, giving us sneaky ideas about how to proceed. Because the first thing our brain does when we see someone we like is release phenylethylamine. Big fancy word, huh? Phenylethylamine is literally the first spark to fly when we feel attracted to someone, setting off fireworks of norepinephrine and dopamine. Norepinephrine gets our adrenaline going, hence your sexy sweaty palms and flushed cheeks, and dopamine gives you that "I've never been happier" feeling. Essentially your nervous system goes into high-drive, pumping adrenaline and estrogen like an open fire hydrant, and your brain says, "Don't it feel good?"

But here's the thing: your brain is a big fat liar. As soon as the adrenaline kicks in, you start ignoring the rules. "Oh, this guy's different," you say.

Until he's not.

Here's the hard truth. As long as he has a penis, he's wired just like every other guy. And as long as he's alive in the twenty-first century, he's probably going to respond like every other guy. Hand it all over in the first two weeks, and there won't be much reason for him to stay interested. Take it slow. Keep your distance. Keep him curious, and you'll keep him interested.

And that, my friends, is what Week Two is all about.

FUN FACT: Your brain is a big fat liar. As soon as the adrenaline kicks in, you start ignoring the rules. "Oh, this guy's different," you say. Right. Take it slow. Keep your distance. Keep him curious, and you'll keep him interested.

Stop the Story

The first step is to keep busy so that you can "stop the story" we all create in our heads. You know the story. Heck, *I* know the story. One of the last guys I dated, Andrew, was younger than me. He was so cute and charming that I ignored the fact that young guys haven't generally worked out for me. Andrew was a publicist who I met through a friend, and though he preferred to text rather than talk and took his time contacting me, by the end of the second date I already saw us walking down the aisle together. Like me, Andrew often put work first, but told me on our first date that he wanted to find someone who would get him out of the office and into the world more. I felt like he was reading my mind, convinced that we had *so* much in common, there was no way we weren't going to end up together. And though he still wasn't calling, and his texts were less and less frequent, I still couldn't get past my own fantasics to see what was really going on.

Don't try to pretend that you haven't gotten lost in the story, imagining things that are far from happening and obsessing about what might not happen. Men can sense that from a mile away, and that's not a good thing. Because the kind of man you want to be with stays occupied with work and friends and hobbies, and you need to do the same thing. Don't spend your time in Fantasyland, or worse, waiting for his call. Trust me, it won't turn out well. It never does.

Ever hear the story of the girl who was blindsided? Well, I have. Every day. And it's not like that Sandra Bullock movie—no football scholarships here.

Recently my client Tarina went through the blind side. Things were going great with Tarina's guy Derrick. Everything felt right. He was into her. She was into him. So *naturally* (her word, not mine) they became intimate. Everything felt so right. It was passionate. Mind-blowing! Derrick even cooked breakfast. And then, out of the blue, this great guy pulls back and it's on the fast track to over.

It's time to rethink "out of the blue."

Let's backtrack. Sure, Tarina was mysterious and guarded on that first date. She was casual and fun on the second. But then she hit date three, and whether she realized it or not, things changed. She was suddenly making plans for them to go see her friend's play the next week. She was texting him in the middle of the day to see how he was doing. She was buying into a story that wasn't even written yet, and she was losing the control that, as a woman, is rightly hers. And yours.

Because that's the thing: We are in control, until we start losing our marbles and giving it away. Men know that we have the control, and they respect us for it, which is why they get just as confused when we start handing it over on date three. But here's the kicker: The minute he knows you're trying to control the situation, you are no longer in control. We're kind of like the Great Oz, pulling the strings from behind the green curtain, but then when we emerge, forcing whatever next step is ahead, the guys run. This is why you don't initiate. You don't set up the dates. You don't call first. You don't text first. And you do not under any circumstances become friends on Facebook.

Date Like *This*: Why You Need to Hold the Reins

You don't need to be aloof or act uninterested but you do need to keep your cool. Recently, my best friend Danielle was on a third date. She had really begun to like Thomas. Sure, he was younger than her (okay, okay, so it didn't work for Demi, either), but they were having a great time, and even though she knows every rule in the book—she's best friends with me after all—she still thought, "This time is different."

So while Thomas was busy paying the check, she was getting ready to ask her big question. "So . . ."

He looked up and she could see him brace himself.

But good ole Danielle continued, ignoring his reaction, "Would you like to come to my friend's birthday party next week? It'll be really low-key. It's just at a bar downtown and there should be a lot of people and . . ."

He interrupted her rambling. "Sure." Then he smiled briefly and stood up. "You ready to go?"

She tried to pretend that his reply was enthusiastic. Immediately after the date, she called me to say that he seemed excited to meet her friends. She ignored his short response and quick getaway. Three days later, Thomas dumped her.

Now, was that because she asked him out? Maybe not. It wouldn't have been the end of the world had he met her friends, and certainly, she had every right to say yes had he asked her the same. But by trying to initiate on date three, she basically took those very powerful reins and handed them right over to Thomas. If you have ever ridden a horse you know what happens next: They run. And so Thomas ran. Stop giving men that opportunity and they will actually stay.

Not Like *That*: Why You Shouldn't Listen to Your Heart

When it comes to work, when it comes to family, and later, hopefully, when it comes to your love life, it is important to listen to your heart. When it comes to the first eight weeks of dating, ignore your heart entirely. It is influenced by the nasty chemicals in your brain, which convince you that you have found the love of your life and that the feeling is mutual. It really is simple science.

FUN FACT: The reason attraction is so mind-altering is that when you like someone your brain releases dopamine, the same chemical that cocaine triggers. It's no wonder people say they are high on love—they are!

And just as you wouldn't trust someone who is high on drugs, you can't trust yourself when you've got all those chemicals firing. It's like that old "Just Say No" commercial where they crack an egg on a sizzling skillet, and say, "This is your brain on drugs." Well, it's also your brain on love.

It is this sort of thinking that makes us believe that it's perfectly okay to ask a guy out to our friend's birthday party on the third date. Much as we joke that men have two brains, so do we. We have the smart one that gets us good jobs and helps us save money. And then there is our other brain. This is the part of us that falls in "love" by date three. It tells us that the man we are dating likes us so it doesn't matter whether we ask him out or initiate a serious kiss. This brain cries, "It's not like we're in the '50s!"

But you know what? Human brains haven't changed since the 1950s. Just as you are battling chemistry, so is that man who you believe is falling in love with you. But his hormones tell a different story. Flooded with testosterone, he feels he has made his conquest and no longer needs to hunt for your attention. As soon as you hand over those reins, your "heart" has failed you. You can keep yourself from making the wrong move. Run your "great" ideas by three friends, and make sure one of them is a straight man. This is no time for feminine intuition. It is time for cool and rational behavior where you follow these simple guidelines and you ask others for guidance . . . and not your heart.

Don't Put All Your Eggs in One Basket

When we make a guy number one he can feel it. You can play it as cool as you want to, but if you're spending all your energy thinking about him, he knows. And it will scare him away. It's not that men want us to be aloof; they just get freaked out when after three dates, we focus all of our attention on them. Who wants that kind of responsibility when you're only just getting to know each other? No one.

That is why putting all of your eggs in one basket is a

surefire way to make a man run. You must stay busy. You must keep dating. And even if it's the case, which it shouldn't be, don't ever bring up the fact that you aren't seeing anyone else! By the time you have made it to date three with Guy #1, you should be going on date one with Guy #2. Which means you should keep that dating profile active online, you should ask your friends about any single guys they might know, you should give out your number when asked, and still go out with friends and flirt with guys. Your dating life is not closed for business. Keep your options open, and you'll find that not only will you be less obsessed, but you'll also be better able to keep your head attached to your shoulders.

Dating and feeling chemistry with someone is an exciting process, but you also need to hold that excitement back—like in handcuffs. Trust me, if you spread your energy around, instead of devoting it all to one guy, you will quickly find out who is worth dating, and who is worth amputating.

Date Like *This*: Just Keep Dating

In the middle of a busy afternoon, I got a call from my client Tarina. She had just gone on her fourth date in two weeks with Michael. Tarina is a thirty-something nutritionist with a stellar body and a heart of gold. And she is exhausted by people constantly asking her how she hasn't found a man yet.

"They act like it's all my fault. Like maybe I have some secret flaw that keeps the men away. I don't! It's just every time I like someone they seem to disappear."

When Tarina called me, she was gushing. She couldn't stop talking about Michael—how sweet he was, how good-looking, how smart and funny and kind. Her voice got quiet as she finally said, "I feel like I've finally met the right guy."

To which I replied, "Then don't stop looking."

As I explained to Tarina, the minute you start liking someone, go on a date with someone else. Stay out there! Keep dating. You are not, nor should you be, exclusive by Week Two. And as great as Guy #1 might seem, you are still getting to know him. You need to keep playing the field for two reasons: one, to get some perspective on what makes you so gaga in the first place, and two, to keep yourself distracted so you don't start thinking, "I've finally met the right guy."

Two days later, Tarina went on a date with George, and though she wasn't as wowed as she was with Michael, it helped her to pace the other relationship. She explained to me later, "Since I was dating more than one guy, I didn't feel comfortable being intimate with either of them. It really allowed me to get to know a couple of different people at once, and though I still really like Michael, I didn't find myself obsessing as much."

Not Like *That*: Don't Give Anyone Top Billing

One of the biggest takeaways I've learned from matchmaking is that men have trouble stopping the story, and some of them find the "don't put your eggs in one basket" rule a little too challenging. I have had so many male clients fall in love by the end of their first date and then blow it. Recently, I worked with a finance attorney from Connecticut who had divorced the previous year and was ready to start dating again. Adam is more on the nerdy side, but still a good-looking guy with thick brown hair and a lanky frame. He used to play high school basketball and still plays with friends on the weekend.

I knew he wanted someone who was also athletic. His ex was never interested in joining his workouts and that annoyed him. So I set him up with Kathleen, a marathon runner and real estate agent. Kathleen has been single for some time, and also said she was hoping to find someone that she could share her hobbies with. I thought I had a real match. And at first, so did they. After the first date, Kathleen wrote me, saying, "Adam was sweet, fun, and had a lot of energy. He is definitely super-smart, which was intimidating, but he didn't seem to take himself too seriously."

Good, I thought. This could go somewhere. Then I got Adam's feedback. He wrote me, "Thank you, thank you, Amy. I have found my future wife. Kathleen is exactly what I have been looking for in a woman. She's smart and a great listener. She seemed really comfortable with herself. I could see us going for long bike rides along the Hudson. And was already thinking she might like to go to France with me during the summer."

To which I replied, "Adam. Slow down. It's November." I have to admit, I was worried. Adam wasn't dating anyone else and had given Kathleen top billing, and I knew where that could lead.

Sadly, Adam didn't slow down, and though Kathleen did her best to give him a fighting chance, Adam's thinking of the future got in his way. He came off as aggressive as opposed to romantic, and when he mentioned the France idea (oh, Adam!) on their third date, Kathleen got nervous. She wrote me later:

From: Kathleen
Subject: Adam

Okay, so I got your message about Adam. He is asking you about me, isn't he? Why is it that the guys I like all run? And that all guys that like me are crazy? I'm sorry to say that about Adam, but he was so hyper the other night, talking about all the things we were going to do. I think he even invited me to France. He seems like a nice guy and I know he's new to dating again, but it was too much. I felt like I was on a date with an excited puppy. Maybe we can try with someone who has been dating for longer?

—K

Date Like *This*: Set the Pace

A few months back, I was talking to a guy friend when he confided that he normally sleeps with girls by the third or fourth date.

"Third or fourth date?" I practically cried. "Do you even know her middle name by then?"

"Why would I need to know her middle name?" He laughed. "I'm just sleeping with her."

Exactly. If you are getting intimate by the third or fourth date, the guy in question is probably "just sleeping" with you. It is your job to hold back. I know we all get a little frazzled here. How come guys don't have to do this? Why is it our job? We are liberated women who should be able to sleep with whom we want when we want!

And we are. But if you are a liberated woman who wants to be in a relationship, then you need to set the pace. Because the truth is, we don't have a penis. We do not contend with a brain full of hormones that tells us we need to have sex with as many people as possible so that the human race will multiply. We are not interested in "spreading our seed." And once a man gets to know you, once he begins to bond, he won't be, either. But at the beginning, he isn't bonded to you. He isn't even exclusively dating you. So instead of becoming a location stop on his tour, make him stop and pay attention to who you are.

Men bond emotionally, too, but if sex comes too quickly, they will no longer have the need.

This is why you have to set the pace. Kissing is an amazing thing. Like most activities on the planet, the more you do it, the better you become. There is no reason why during your first early weeks, you cannot end each date with a kiss. Sure, they'll probably get heavier and hotter (as they should) but as you learn more about each other, they'll also become more interesting, even more romantic.

Instead of focusing on physical intimacy, you will also develop an emotional connection. The kind where someone knows your middle name before he sleeps with you.

Not Like *That*: Just Say Yes

One of my clients, Bree, recently wrote me after her date with Bryan. Bree is a landscape architect in Los Angeles, and Bryan is a movie executive. They both professed a great love of the outdoors and the desire to find a committed and stable relationship. Their first date went well, so I had high hopes for them in their second week, until I got this e-mail from Bree:

From: Bree
Subject: Bryan

Bryan and I had our second date last Thursday. I ended up asking him to take me home because he kept talking about sex and it was making me uncomfortable. The last straw was when he asked if I'd ever had a bisexual experience. . . . It was only our second date! He left a voice mail the next day to apologize and said he hoped we could be friends, and I texted back to say of course I would think of him as a friend . . . so no hard feelings, but no more dates, either.:)

Bryan, Bryan, Bryan. Bringing up sex on a second date is a no-no. Thankfully, Bree is a smart girl and could see the signs loud and clear. If you are on a date where all the guy does is talk about sex, go home. He is not worth dating.

No matter how the subject comes up—whether it's a natural segue or dominating and rude as in Bryan's case—sex should never be a topic on the second, third, or even the fourth date. If your date skews the conversation in that direction, you can just as easily skew it away. Bring up another topic, and don't respond to any further mention of the nasty.

By showing that you're not interested in discussing it at this juncture, you put some distance between you and sexy time. This is called setting boundaries, and it's a crucial part of dating. You are negotiating the rules here, and if you give him an inch ("It's okay to talk dirty just as long as I don't do anything about it"), it will quickly turn into a mile ("Oops, how did we just have sex?").

You are worth your date getting to know you, and having feelings for you, before you ever talk about S-E-X. And if your date isn't comfortable with that, then you know he probably isn't someone worth waiting for.

---

pace *n.*: a rate of movement, especially in stepping, walking, dating, etc.; the way you direct the progress of the relationship by staying in charge.

Watch for the Signs of Bullshit

Have you ever heard about a friend or a coworker's cousin who came home to find her boyfriend's e-mail account open and messages to other women on it? You shake your head in pity and judgment, asking, "How could she not have seen the signs?" Simple, she was into the guy. And when we're into someone, we're not always good at seeing signs. In fact, even if those signs are there, right in front of us, in blinking red lights, we have a tendency to drive right through them. This is why we need to hold the reins, set the pace, keep our distance, stay out there dating, and hold true to our boundaries, because it's really hard to see the forest for the trees when you've got your nose pressed up against the bark.

Unfortunately, not everyone is going to be obvious with his signs. In fact, their strange tics or quirks might seem charming at first. Stay alert. Pay attention to what he says, how he behaves around other women, and whether he is paying attention to you. There are plenty of narcissists out there, and though not all of them are serial cheaters, many of them will break your heart. A lot of women get flattered by the positive aspects of a man, and refuse to see all the negatives, only to admit later that they knew something was wrong all along.

I could write a hundred pages about all the things guys do to show that they just aren't into you. Oh wait, that's been done. Then why are you still buying the bullshit? During Week Two, you are still giving someone the benefit of the doubt. Don't kick him to the curb for any little infraction, but do make note when he's handing you a bunch of b.s.

Date Like *This*: Stay Alert

My friend Robin recently dated a guy whose confidence was intoxicating. The hostesses knew him at fancy restaurants, where he would plunk down a hefty tip with a wink and the grace of a ballroom dancer. Jacob opened doors, paid for Robin's cab rides home, and even sent flowers after their second date. Robin was duly impressed. But she did her best to stay objective.

On their fourth date, Robin got up to use the restroom. Jacob rose with her and gave her a peck on the cheek, as though to say he would miss her when she was gone. When she got to the restroom, she realized that she had left her purse at the table. As she rounded the corner to the main dining room of the restaurant, she saw the hostess, whom he seemed to know so well, leaning seductively over Jacob. He laughed and touched the woman's leg in a way that seemed *way* too familiar. Robin could have told herself that he was just friends with the woman. Hell, she could have lied to herself and made them first cousins. But she didn't. She walked up to the table, got her purse, and left.

Later, she told me, "I don't want a guy that acts like that. I want someone who only wants to touch *my* leg. And to do that while he thought I was in the restroom. Gross."

Not Like *That*: Don't Buy the Bullshit

We've all done it, but if we want to be with the right guy, we need to stop making excuses for the wrong ones. Last fall, I got a call from one of my former clients, Brooke. Brooke was a writer who met her last boyfriend through me, and after their breakup she had been dating on her own. Unfortunately, she was having some trouble. She had gone on an amazing first date with Micah. Micah was a pediatrician, and though doctors are known to have crazy work hours, he told her he was really trying to create some balance in his life because he wanted a relationship. He even said, "I treat kids all day, but I would like to have some of my own in the future." Sigh . . .

After their first date, they continued texting every day. (Yes, texting. Sigh . . .) But as they entered Week Two, he still hadn't asked her out. That's when she called me, and pleaded, "He's busy, right? He is a freaking doctor." I listened as she continued making excuses, knowing that she wasn't reaching out to me because she wanted me to agree with them. Instead I asked her, "If he has so much time to text you cute little reminders of his existence, why doesn't he have the time to set another date?"

"Why hasn't he called?" I'm asked that question constantly. The truth is it doesn't matter *how* busy a man is, if he's *truly* interested in having a relationship with you, he'll call to plan the second date very shortly thereafter.

BULLSHIT BAROMETER

Men do not leave women in the dark if they want to continue dating them. They do leave you in the dark, however, if they are keeping you on the back burner to see if something better comes along. So stop kidding yourself and look out for the signs of bullshit.

EIGHT SIGNS OF BULLSHIT

1. He says he's going to call and he doesn't.
2. He hasn't asked you out again or hasn't set another date.
3. He says he's really busy but doesn't tell you when he won't be.
4. He only sends texts and never calls you.
5. You hear from him sporadically—once a week or even less.
6. He cancels dates or tries to ask you out at the last minute.
7. He sends you long e-mails but doesn't try to see you.
8. You get the feeling that he might be dating someone else . . . exclusively.

Even if his schedule is insane, and he really isn't able to do it right away, he will still bring it up and say something like, "I had a great time with you the other night. Just wanted to let you know my work has me jumping through hoops over the next seven days but I can't wait to see you! Maybe we can get together the week after if that works for you."

I promise, if he is interested, he will try to set a date.

As much as Mr. Pediatrician seemed like a great guy, Brooke had to face the fact that he was letting her hang out in second place. You should not be put in second place while some guy plays the field.

If a guy likes you, you will know. So do not fall into the trap of making excuses. Because once you start allowing bad behavior to slide, it's no longer his fault—it's yours. Like they say, fool me once, shame on you. Fool me twice, shame on me.

Date Like *This*: Have Fun

Okay, okay. I'm sure by this point, you're saying, "If I have to do all of this to get a man, I'm not interested." And I get it. But the fact is, it really does come down to just a few simple rules that anyone can apply. Every mammal does a mating dance. Be yourself, do what you like, just abide by that week's simple rules. And pretty soon, you'll be relaxing and having fun on your dates. You won't freak out over every little detail or sign. And you won't judge the date while you're on it because you'll have set aside time for that afterward, when you're home and removed from the source of your interest, or lack thereof. But in the moment, when you're sitting across the table, have fun!

Not Like *That*: Stop Hating on Dating

We are walking through an eight-week program here. The rules will not be this stringent once you're married and yelling at each other from across your three-bedroom house. This is not a crash diet. These are just simple steps about how to date that will soon become second nature. In fact, you won't be able to imagine having dated any other way! And yes, *at first* it's not easy. Some of the rules you will not be happy about following. You will be tempted to lie to yourself, and say, "It's okay if just this once I make an exception." Don't. Dating is hard when you are learning, but if you keep practicing, you (and it) will get better.

I have a good friend who opens practically every date, saying, "I hate dating." That's like going into an interview and telling them you hate their company. "Well, I'm not saying I hate them!" she explained.

But she is. If you're on a date, it means you are both in the act of dating. To say you don't like to date means you'd rather be home eating low-fat popcorn out of a plastic bowl with your moisturizing mask on than be out meeting someone new.

If you expect that you're not going to have a good time, you probably won't. Stop hating on dating because it's not actually the dating you hate, it's the fact that you're vulnerable and have fumbled through dating thus far. But if you're going into it with a *clear* head and your feet *on the ground,*

> We have all been frustrated one too many times, often walking into dates with low expectations. But be careful what you wish for, because you might just get it.

then who says you need to be vulnerable? Even if the date is a bust, you can go home and see what you learned from it.

Quiz yourself afterward:

- Was I interested in what my date had to say?
- What about him did I like?
- What about him didn't I like?
- What could I have done better?
- What did I do well?
- Would I like to go out with him again?

WEEK TWO: CHOOSE YOUR OWN RELATIONSHIP

The one thing you need to hold foremost in your mind is this: You are in control. Men know this, but women have a tendency to forget. When we meet someone we like, we often throw that important tool out the window—handing men all of our power and all of our precious cards. And then we wonder why he gets bored and moves on after only a couple of dates. It is you who must hold the reins and set the pace, creating the foundation for what could possibly be a healthy and romantic relationship. You are a catch—know that, even with all of your quirks and funny features and flaws—and that there is a great guy out there waiting for you, but he needs to prove that he's a catch, too. You don't need to pretend he's something more than he is and you don't need to date someone who doesn't want to be dating you. Assert your position as #1 by not making him *your* #1. Get out there and date, have fun, enjoy the experience, and you will find that the dating game is not a chore at all, but rather a really great hobby.

Eight Steps to Everlasting

1. Hold the reins if you don't want him to run.
2. Don't listen to your heart, yet . . .
3. Keep dating. Go out with friends, keep your online profile up, and don't stop flirting. Don't put all your eggs in his basket.

4. Set the pace—both in terms of how much you see each other and how much you do when you're together. Remember, just say no.
5. Stay away from daydreaming about what could be, don't buy the bullshit about what is, and keep busy so you can "stop the story."
6. Do not become friends on Facebook.
7. If you want to call, text, or stop by his work to say hi after that date, be sure to run your "great" idea by three friends, and make sure one of them is a straight man.
8. Stop hating on dating.

Week Three

Learning to Read Him

Love or Lust?

Okay, so you've been holding the reins with a firm and flexible grip. He's been showing all the right behaviors and you're having fun together. In fact, you're feeling pretty good. Great! But don't lose that control now, whatever you do, because this third week is when women tend to trip up most, making choices that can ruin an otherwise awesome experience. Don't get too comfortable. And don't start acting overly confident. Your work is not done yet. In fact, it's really just beginning.

Week three is a turning point for both of you, the stage when you figure out if you want to invest more energy in this young relationship. Spending time or wasting time—it's up to you.

Whether you're aware of it or not, your date is paying attention to your cues. That means he's reading you to figure out what kind of woman you are, and he's making some major decisions based on that reading. If you've been setting the pace and keeping your distance, he's probably intrigued, wondering what's beyond your casual reserve and easygoing nature. He's also trying to figure out where this relationship is headed: into the bedroom, into something more serious, or into its final week.

This week is about whether you're falling in love or falling in lust. I know it's very early to talk about love—but we're talking about *falling* in love. Not *being* in love. Two very different things. This third week is about those nervous, heart-pumping jitters that precede the Big L—not about picking a china pattern. For some people, the Big L means a serious, exclusive relationship filled with vacations and mutual friends, and though they may not be ready for it right this minute, they definitely see it heading in that direction. For others, the Big L means Lust—it's all about feeling good, and little else.

FUN FACT: Falling in love is not the same as being in love. Attraction releases one set of neurochemicals, that trifecta of fire-starter phenylethylamine, nerve-wracking adrenaline, and feel-good dopamine. But love releases its own cocktail, bonding us emotionally to the other person in a much deeper way. Lust says we need to get it on because it will feel good. Love says we need to create a life together.

As you move into Week Three, take the time to see how things are shaping up between the two of you. Of course, not everything needs to be in perfect order for a relationship to work. Sometimes, men have real reasons for not always doing the right thing. And one of the main reasons is that they simply don't know how. Like you, they weren't taught properly how to date. That doesn't mean you should suffer bad behaviors. But you should try to be open and honest.

That said, there are some absolutes. If it's clear that all the guy wants is sex, get out. If it's clear that you are only a weekday girl and that's not changing, get out. If spending time with your new man makes you feel less than, or degraded, then get the heck out. And if you're tempted to look the other way when he disappoints you by what he says or what he does, if you're tempted to say, "Well, maybe he just . . . ," then stop yourself. Maybe is the town that Denial lives in. In fact, Denial is its mayor.

Identifying the Signs

Too often we project our own feelings onto the guy we're dating. We want so much to make the relationship work that sometimes we turn a blind eye to what's really going on. We come up with reasons why he's acting a certain way and then invent justifications for a relationship we know isn't going in the right direction. Likewise, we take ourselves out of the equation by imagining that love or lust is just the result of a dozen random things that have nothing to do with us. He's in love or he isn't. He's in lust or he isn't. Not true. You can't change a guy, of course, but you can influence how he acts. And those actions have a direct correlation to his feelings. It's that whole cause-and-effect thing, and it can be mighty empowering.

The empowering part here is that your actions play a major role in which way the Big L swings. That's right. Based on his behaviors (and yours), you can sway the jury in either favor. But first you need to be able to read the signs. And believe me, by week three, the signs are there. So the question now is, is he falling in love or he is falling in lust? And what can you do to make the right one happen?

---

love *n.*: a profoundly tender, passionate affection for another person; sexual passion or desire, the subject of poetry, love songs, and late-night phone calls, not to be confused with *lust.*

A guy who regularly makes plans to see you, who makes a conscious effort for you to feel special is definitely falling in love. My friend Tim is a good example. He was really falling for a new girl, so he'd ask her out on a Monday for Thursday or Friday night. Not only would he ask what day she was available, but he would find out what time was good for her and what she might like to do—he wanted to make sure he was going to see her. Tim's actions spoke of a man who was falling in love. He was interested in seeing his new lady because he enjoyed spending time with her. She made him laugh. He liked hearing about her life. He appreciated that she liked hearing about his. He went out of his way to make sure he made a good impression, and cared about what she thought of him. He wasn't just taking a shot. He was taking careful and precise action to get what he wanted: a relationship with this new woman.

There were no excuses. There were no games. And there was no bullshit. He liked her and he made sure she knew it. And at this point, you should know it, too.

So let's take stock of where you are.

By now, you should be seeing him about twice a week, and when you don't see each other, he should be in touch by phone, either calling or texting a simple "Hey, how's your day going?" Though not all conversations should be taking place in texts, it's okay for him to send one or two. Be wary though if that's all he does. The texts should be just one ingredient in his way to woo you, showing that he is thinking about you, and is not afraid to show it.

I remember asking Tim what the difference was between dating a girl he was falling for, and one that he wasn't.

He laughed. "That's easy. When I like someone, I go out of my way to make sure they know it. I don't want them to be confused or to think I'm playing games. I shoot straight when I want a girl."

> If a guy is into you, he will take action to show he cares. He will listen to you at dinner, and remember what you've said. If you say that you love Indian food, that will be your next date. He will want to impress you. Let him.

I followed by asking, "So what happens when you don't?"

Tim looked down, clearly embarrassed. "Well, if I'm not sure, I act unsure. I mean I'll still call, but just enough to stay in touch. I figure it's worth checking out, but I'm not going to put a lot of energy into it."

You are worth the energy.

I have to admit I love Week Three. It's filled with possibility and the hope of what might be. This is when your guy should be inviting you to more intimate affairs, or scheduling a solid week in advance. By Week Three, you should both be figuring out whether you see this continuing into Week Four and Week Five. I *never* suggest setting future plans until this point, but now is when you begin to see a future, even if it's only two weeks away. By inviting you to his friend's birthday party the following week or an art exhibit that's opening at the end of the month, he is showing that not only does he want to continue spending time with you, he's planning on it.

If you feel like he's distracted or simply not that interested, make note of it and watch what happens next. He might be keeping his options open—fine for a business transaction, but not for a relationship.

Take an honest look at whether he is treating you like a man falling in love . . . or lust. Here are eight questions to ask yourself:

1. How often does he call?
2. How often do you see each other?
3. Is he putting energy into making sure he gets face time with you?
4. Does he reach out to you on the days that you don't see each other?
5. Is he making plans a week or two into the future?
6. Do you feel that he is thinking about you?
7. Is he acting unsure, failing to call, and allowing days to pass with no communication?
8. Are you feeling honored or ignored?

He's Falling in Love *If* . . .

So you're spending the day bike riding through the park. Afterward you go to lunch, and as you sit across from your date, you notice he has begun to ask you more intimate questions—nothing prying or rude, but questions about your parents and your siblings. He is showing a genuine interest in your life and the people in it, whether he has met them or not.

Many of us have gotten used to dating the guy who is into himself, who seems to be in another world as we talk about our lives and dreams. That is not a man in love. A man in love asks questions, he wants to find out more. You intrigue him and he finds your stories and experiences entertaining. This is not someone who listens halfheartedly, but rather someone who pays attention.

And you deserve that. I hope you are beginning to see that this quest is not just about getting a guy, but rather about getting a guy who cares about you, and who deserves your affection. If you're talking and the person across the table isn't listening, amputate and run. He will never listen. Even if the relationship continues, you will find yourself feeling isolated and unloved, questioning why you ever started dating this person in the first place. Don't waste your time on someone who doesn't care about what you have to say. Look out for someone who asks the right questions, who remembers what you said on your second date. Pay attention to these small details—they are *loud* signs.

He's Falling in Lust *If*. . .

When Tanya called me on a Monday morning, I could tell she had been crying. A graduate student studying to be a child psychologist, Tanya knows more about the human mind than most people, but when it comes to dating, all that knowledge flies out the window. For the last three weeks she had been dating Lawrence, an account executive at an insurance company in Miami. At first things were going great. They were going out to dinner twice a week. He even went to a birthday party for one of her friends, charming her girls and in general behaving like the perfect gentleman. But by the end of Week Three, Tanya began to notice a disturbing trend.

From: Tanya
Subject: Lawrence

Hey Amy,
Thanks for listening to me today. The more I think about it, I guess I'm just frustrated that I feel like I found this perfect guy but then he won't share anything about himself with me. It's like on paper everything makes sense, and I know we're both physically attracted to each other! But then we sit down and all he does is make jokes or chat about pop culture and music and other stuff. I don't even think he's asked me if I have brothers or sisters or anything yet. Also, he never seems to ask me out for the weekends—it's always after work or on a Friday night. I'd like some day dates by now. Should I be concerned? Or am I just being picky? Dating is so hard!

XO,
Tanya

Though I didn't, and wouldn't, tell Tanya to give up all hope at this point, I would say to be wary. The third week can be an interesting gray zone—some men take a little longer to open up, to share their lives with you, or to even ask about yours. But chances are, if he's met your friends and you haven't met any of his, there's an issue. Likewise, if he's keeping the conversation super casual, neglecting to talk about his personal life, there's an issue. And if he hasn't asked you out yet for the weekend or a date during the day, there's an issue.

If he's treating your dates with the same care and concern that he would with hitting the gym after work, he's in lust with you, not in love.

I wrote Tanya back that day and told her to stick it out another week or so. I even suggested telling him that she was busy during the week with work, but had some free time on Saturday afternoon if he wanted to see her. I explained that she needed to take action in order to stop herself from becoming the weekday girl. She needed to stop saying "yes" to weekday invites, explaining that she was really busy during the week but that she thought she might have some free time on the weekend. That doesn't mean that Tanya should take any date offered (she should have her weekends busy after all), but she should negotiate herself out of the easy dinner or drinks routine.

You need to determine whether that's what he's doing, and you need to try to stop it. You can potentially still reverse the fate of the relationship. But if he only wants you as a weekday woman, then amputate now.

Dating ADD

If your guy consistently reaches out to you the same day to make plans, or if he's consistently seeing what "you're up to" that night, he's not that serious about you. Or worse, he's got a case of Dating ADD.

There is a difference between someone who is interested in you but is still going out with a couple of other women, and someone who can't choose between the women he's dating. If you don't feel like you're number one, or if this man has a history of dating many women without ever committing to one, then you need to decide whether he is someone you want to be with. And you need to take a hard look at yourself and make sure you're not doing the same.

Yes, you should be continuing to go out on other dates, but by Week Three, you should be getting a sense of which man you want to be with. Just as you don't want to be lumped in with the rest, you shouldn't be lumping him in with the rest, either. You can see other men and still pick a favorite. So ask yourself: Is he your favorite? And is he treating you like you're his?

A lot of men go from woman to woman—every freaking night—and are incapable of focusing on just one. If you think you're dating a "Dating ADD," cut him loose. Now!

There are ways you can (and should) take action so you don't get lost in the mix. Once you're in an exclusive relationship, there are going to be many casual, last-minute dates, but that's still a no-no at this point. *Don't* agree to go on them. If a guy asks you out for that same evening, say it's too last-minute for you, or tell him you already have plans. Nothing piques a guy's interest more than to think that you're too busy to see him. And nothing shows him more that you're not a last-minute kind of gal than by refusing to be that kind of woman. If you shut down his careless efforts, he will either move on (and good riddance to him if so), or he will start changing his tune . . . away from lust and into love.

He's Falling in Love *If . . .*

Just recently, I set up my clients Marta and Jason. Marta is an Italian food publicist who loves tall men, and Jason is a talent agent who is tall and loves foreign women (not to mention food), so when they met, it was a pretty easy connection. After a couple of weeks, Jason invited her to an awards party. He explained that it was a big to-do and would be a lot of fun. Though Marta was excited, she maintained her composure.

"I would love to, but let me check my schedule," she replied. "Give me a call tomorrow and I'll let you know."

By taking that little time out, not to mention playing it cool and making sure that he called her the next day to confirm, she proved herself to be a distance maker, not a desperate I'll-take-what-I-can-get kind of girl.

The night of the awards party, she met Jason at a restaurant up the street from the event, where they had an early dinner and then headed over. He made the plan and took the lead in setting everything up. She told me later, "We were both dressed to the nines, and he had already given me flowers. As we walked into the party, he put his hand on the small of my back, and whispered to me, 'You are the most beautiful woman here,' and I knew I was there as his very special date."

He's Falling in Lust *If* . . .

We've all been here. You're going on amazing dates. You're having a lot of fun, but then you don't hear from him for a couple of days, or a week goes by before you see him again. Though it's perfectly normal for a guy to pull back a little at this point, he should also be making simple gestures to show he's still interested. You may feel like you're driving a stalled car, waiting for the engine to turn back on, and frustrated that you're not getting as far along as you would like. But don't blow the horn just yet.

FUN FACT: Being a guy is *not* a medical condition—it's not amnesia that prevents him from calling.

Recently, I was sitting at lunch with Maxine, one of my closest friends from college. She barely touched her salad as she whined, "But we have so much fun when we're together. I don't get it. He tells me how beautiful I am, and how I make him laugh. But then when we're not together, it's like he forgets about me. Do you think it could be a medical condition?"

"I don't think being a guy is a medical condition," I reply.

"No, like amnesia or dementia or something," Maxine says. And we wonder what the heck is wrong with us?

I break it to Maxine that no, she is not dating a guy with short-term memory loss. "It's not like he's Drew Barrymore in *50 First Dates*," I explain. "He's probably just pulling back a little. When was the last time he called?"

Maxine looks down. "Two weeks."

I feel her pain because I have often prayed that my man is suffering from a serious mental disorder rather than face the truth that he is not a man falling in love. And if he's not reaching out at all, if he's not setting up dates or not staying in contact in between those dates, then it's probably one of two things: either he's not that serious, or he's dating other people—and he's not that serious.

He's Falling in Love *If*. . .

It was Eilene and Bill's third week of dating. I hadn't heard from Bill in over a week so I decided to check in. It's amazing what men will tell me. As a matchmaker, I am the perfect neutral voice, and they trust that the feedback they offer me, good or bad, will be put to good use. And it is. I'm using that feedback here to help all of you learn how to date. As you're beginning to see, these steps are not based on some arbitrary and outdated rules, but rather on what men are really looking for in women. Real men such as my male clients. Real men that I talk to and work with every day. Bill's e-mail was clearly written by a real man falling in real love.

> *From: Bill*
> *Subject: DATE #4 Eilene*
>
> *I feel like I'm really getting to know Eilene because we talk a lot about family and what we both want out of life. We went to the zoo in the park and ended up spending the whole day walking around. We talked a lot about her life experiences thus far, having been married so young and how that has affected her. She said she's always just been happier in a solid relationship. It's funny, because I feel the same way. It was really, really nice seeing her again.* I really *like her. We both agreed that we have something unique going on—a little magic perhaps. . . . I think I should put my membership with you on hold because I don't want to meet anyone else. I just want to see where things go with Eilene. She's really special.*
>
> *Bill*

I love these e-mails! If a guy suggests spending time together during the day, moving on from nighttime dates or drinks, he is reaching out for a more serious relationship. Bill wanted to spend time with Eilene. It wasn't about having martinis or seeing her in a candlelit glow; he wanted to know who she was by day. He wanted to spend time in the park, talking one on one. When someone includes you in a daytime activity, asking to get together on a Sunday afternoon or inviting you to brunch on Saturday (without spending the night before!), that is a man who wants to spend real, quality time with you. That is a man who is falling in love. As Bill and Eilene went on to do.

He's Falling in Lust *If*. . .

You're probably wondering what happened between my client Marta and the talent agent who took her to the fancy awards show. And at first, in her denial, so did she. Though she started by playing it cool, she ended it by getting too hot. Because that night, after the romantic dinner and the exclusive party, she screwed up . . . big-time. That night, she went home with Jason and pretended they were in Week Seven and not Week Three. All of a sudden the relationship went from a series of nice dinners across town to movies at his place. She wasn't sure why sleeping with him meant they weren't supposed to eat out anymore, but Jason had apparently decided that she was now a "lust" type, and lust does not require dinner beforehand.

Finally, after two weeks of this behavior, she saw where the relationship was heading. She called me, and asked, "Do you think we have become benefit friends?"

"Friends with benefits?" I corrected her, adding, "Yes, Marta, unfortunately, I think you have."

Though she had made a major mistake with Jason, she decided she wasn't going to make it a permanent condition. It was a cold and snowy Saturday day when Jason called her for the last time. He asked if she "wanted to come over and watch a movie." And she knew what that meant.

If by Week Three, you've gone from romantic candlelit dinners to just watching movies at his place, it's time to cut him loose. Because if he's stopped trying to impress you this early, he won't start again.

"Jason, I'm sorry but I'm looking for a little more than a movie," she told him.

"Um, dinner?"

She knew that she was done negotiating. The deal was off and to take some scraps from the table would only be that . . . scraps.

"No. No dinner. I think we have two very different ideas about where this is going, and it would be a waste of our time to continue doing this," Marta replied.

"Okay" was Jason's curt and heartbreaking response.

Was it hard for her? Yes. Did it hurt? Of course. But sometimes, we need to throw in the towel rather than risk hurting ourselves and seriously compromising our self-esteem. Because once you start creating bad habits, it is really hard, if not downright impossible, to go back.

LOVE AND LUST
Both Four-Letter Words

He's falling in love with you *if* he . . .	He's falling in lust with you *if* he . . .
1. makes plans in advance and always makes sure he's going to see you, even if you're both busy	1. makes you feel like a last-minute girl with his "What are you up to tonight?"
2. asks you out during the day, during weekend nights, or with his friends	2. only wants to see you during the week, and rarely includes other people
3. asks you out more—not less—than before	3. has Dating ADD and can't seem to focus on just one woman
4. pays attention to what you say, what you like, and who you are	4. talks only about himself and fails to ask about you
5. appreciates it when you ask questions about his life, and is open and inviting in his response	5. talks too much about sex or always seems to be hinting at the topic
6. goes out of his way to make a good impression	6. is rude to you or impolite—anything from a failure to open doors to criticizing you (or other women) in some way
7. rearranges his schedule to make it work for you, even if it's inconvenient for him	7. keeps you on the back burner, checking in from time to time, but keeping you in second place behind work, friends, or even other dates
8. compliments you—your personality, your mind, your humor, your talents, and of course, your looks	8. compliments you only on your looks, or does so excessively, stressing language like *hot* or *sexy*

He's Falling in Love *If* . . .

I got off the phone with my dentist and realized I was going to need some help. I was having my wisdom teeth removed Friday afternoon, and would need a friend, to take me home. I called one of my closest girl friends, Sonia, who is one of the few people in my life who could care less if I'm high on laughing gas, or slobbering on her shoulder.

Sonia had been dating Scott for a couple of weeks at that point, and had just started going out with him on the weekends as well. When I asked if she could come get me on Friday, she said yes, but I could hear the disappointment in her voice.

"Sonia, if you already have plans, don't worry about it."

"No way, Amy," she replied. "I'm going to be there for you. Plus, who is going to get you chicken soup from EJ's and watch bad eighties movies with you?"

"Well, did you have plans?" I asked.

"I was going to see a movie with Scott, but it's no big deal. Besides, it's a great opportunity for me to keep my distance, remember?"

How could I say no to that? Sure enough, when Sonia called Scott to tell him, he was more than fine with it. In fact, he even said that being a good friend is the most important role we can have. Swoon. And Sonia did. But she kept her cool. She was getting pretty good at this.

On Friday, she told me, "He pointed out that the movie would still be playing on Saturday and that he could easily reschedule his dinner with a friend for Friday. As he put it, his buddy would not be just getting out of oral surgery."

That is a guy falling in love. If he willingly changes plans to accommodate your schedule, whether it's convenient or not, he is someone worth paying attention to. A guy falling in love tries his best to see you. He works to keep your dates. If you must reschedule, he attempts to see you *sooner* rather than later.

Needless to say, Sonia and Scott had a great time on their date Saturday night. He even asked about me. When Sonia told him that I was doing just fine, he said we would all have to get together soon to celebrate. Not only was Scott showing how much he wanted to spend time with Sonia, he was showing her that he wanted to get to know her friends as well. I am happy to say that Scott and Sonia have now been dating for six months. And I've met him a number of times and still very much approve!

He's Falling in Lust *If*. . .

So what happens when you are on your fourth, fifth, sixth date, and the man sitting across from you is telling you for the third time in the first forty minutes of the date how great you look? Sure, your hormones are probably pumping. Adrenaline's kicking in; you're even getting rosy cheeked. But here's the thing: There are hormones and then there are instincts. Your hormones say, "Oh, yes, he likes me. I knew he did." And your instincts say, in a much more quiet but serious voice, "Why does he keep talking about my looks?" Listen to your instincts, and tell your hormones to shut up.

---

lust *n.*: intense desire or appetite; a powerful sexual urge that often masquerades as love, the thing that turns men into teenage boys.

If you remember my client Bryan, the one who asked his date if she ever had a bisexual experience, then you know I was working with a tough one. Part of my job is not only to coach women on how to behave, but also to advise the men. After that inappropriate date with Bree, Bryan told me that he had gotten nervous and thought that asking about her past sexual experiences would be funny. I explained to him that it was creepy, not funny. Definitely not funny. But just as I suggest the ladies do, I decided to give Bryan one more chance. And at first, he did really well.

Pauline is a stylist who works in the film industry, so I thought she and Bryan would be a great match. If nothing else, they shared a certain lifestyle because of their work. And at the beginning, it seemed to go well. They started by going out to dinner for the first few dates, and then Bryan invited her to the racetrack on the weekend. They even got dressed up, pretending they were going to the Kentucky Derby. Pauline wrote me afterward:

From: Pauline
Re: Date #5

So Bryan and I went to the racetrack this weekend. It started out really fun. We dressed all fancy. I even wore a big hat. We looked kind of silly, which was also great—I was excited that he could do that. But then it was like he couldn't stop complimenting me. It wasn't the first time. A couple times on dates I felt a little strange. Like he told me I had the best legs he had ever seen. Three times in one date. And then this weekend he asked me like five times whether I wanted to go to the beach and commented on how I great I must look in a bikini. It's so weird because we have sooooo *much in common and have such a good time. Should I say something?*

xP

I immediately wrote Bryan and asked him why he was so focused on what Pauline looked like. He replied, rather frankly, "I guess I feel like she is more of a casual relationship. I would love to sleep with her, but I'm not sure that there would be much more involved. We had fun, and I think she is a great girl. But she's not someone who I could see myself settling down with. I do think she's gorgeous and I guess I can't help telling her that. She's a hot chick."

She's a hot chick. Not what I want to hear from a client, and certainly not what poor Pauline was looking for. After that round, I knew it was time for me to cut Bryan loose, but unfortunately Pauline didn't take my cue. She dated him for two more months, and then finally wrote me, "I was hoping the relationship would grow into something more. I always think that if I stick it out, men will change."

And I am here to tell you, just as I told her, they won't.

When a man constantly compliments you about your looks, saying how hot you are, how beautiful you are, what a great kisser you are, how much you turn him on, he is not getting to know you, he is busy thinking about what you will look like in bed.

Don't get fooled by the false Romeo.

Of course, you want someone who thinks you're beautiful, but you also want someone who notices how smart you are, or someone who shows how much respect he has for the work you do. And what about all the other accomplishments in your life? If all he does is talk about how great you look, he is a man in lust and not in love.

WEEK THREE: CHOOSE YOUR OWN RELATIONSHIP

Week Three is not about making any fast moves. It's about learning the lessons of Week Two, keeping your cards close, staying busy, dating other people, and refraining from anything more than a good-night kiss. Week Three is about paying attention to how he treats you. If you are willing to keep your head clear, you should be able to get a sense of whether you are dating a man who is falling in love or falling in lust. Depending on which way it's going, you will know what decisions you must make. If the horse is trying to run off, it might be time to pull back on the reins. Don't say yes to every date. Create a little more distance, and hold that guard up even higher until he has proven that he is looking for the right thing. And if he isn't, *do not waste your time*. There is a good man out there, and every minute you spend with the wrong guy, you risk not meeting the right one.

Eight Steps to Everlasting

1. Suggest daytime and weekend dates.
2. Make sure that he doesn't do the majority of the talking.
3. Say no to any dates that sound too easy—no coffee during the day, no last-minute requests, and nothing at his place.
4. Do not agree to the last-minute date. Make him plan ahead.

5. If he asks you out to a special event, do not agree to go right away. Make *him* confirm with you.
6. Keep your priorities—if your friends, family, or work need you, feel free to reschedule. It will show him that your life is not all about him.
7. Don't do any dude dates—no sports bars, heavy drinking, or anything he might do with his friends. Keep things romantic and yourself feminine.
8. Hold back on anything sexual. Keep kissing!

Week Four

It's All About Intimacy (No, Not That Kind)

Is It Time to Get Physical?

This is the week when even the nicest guy might hint a little more loudly for the boom, boom, boom. And this is the week when you have to say no, no, no. Because Week Four is when the boyfriend/girlfriend bond really starts to develop—unless you get ahead of yourself and start becoming too physical. You've been the one in control, determining the pace of the relationship. And you've been directing how he sees you. You're proving that you are not just a fun girl to hang out with, but that you're a potential mate. He's taking you seriously and you're heading down the road that leads to exclusivity—together. But herein lies the challenge. You need to steer the relationship into an emotional direction, and away from the physical. That's not to say that it shouldn't be getting hotter and heavier (and though we'll be discussing this more soon, let's just say that you need to get comfortable on second base), but Week Four is really about developing the most important intimacy of all: emotional intimacy.

Not all roads lead to exclusivity. It's up to you to steer the relationship away from the physical and into emotional territory.

Patience: A Virtue *and* a Strategy

Have you ever played pool? Even if you haven't, chances are you're familiar with the object of the game. That is, to use your cue to shoot the ball into the pocket. It sounds simple, but it's not easy. In fact, it takes a lot of time and practice to get it right. And patience. Sure, you could just grab the ball and throw it into the pocket, but that's not how the game is played. And that's not how the dating game is played, either. You can't force a relationship. You need to be strategic and patient, and you need to learn how to guide the relationship from a short but tangible distance. And trust me, you can learn to sink the eight ball each time.

So about that "patience" I keep talking about. Just exactly how are you supposed to cultivate that? Simple. You sit back and relax. This is not the time to get freaked out if you don't see or even speak to each other every day.

You should be talking more on the phone and e-mailing each other when you're at work, but if you don't hear from him for one day, that *does not* mean it is over.

Too often, when we lose contact for a few minutes we get nervous and start acting stupid. We call, we text, we e-mail. We think we're showing that we're interested or that we're just sending a friendly reminder of our existence. But in the end, the only thing we're showing is our desperation, and that doesn't look pretty on anyone.

Remember the old story about how a guy would ask a girl out, and if she wasn't interested, she would say she was busy washing her hair? Take a cue and be busy "washing your hair" some nights. It doesn't mean you're not interested, but it does mean that you are not making him your number-one priority. And at this point, he should not be your top priority. He is just a guy who you have been seeing for a month. You should still be taking plenty of time for yourself. This will also make the time you have together more special.

Date Like *This*: Learn the Waiting Game

A few years ago, I was dating a sports-show producer who liked it when I played hard to get. Every time I said no to a date, he would up the ante, and become more persistent and more romantic the next time. Around Week Four, Arthur asked me to a movie on a Friday night and I told him that I had plans, explaining, "I could do something on Saturday or Sunday during the day." He agreed to Sunday and then instead of a movie, we went sailing around Manhattan. That was a big lesson for me. I realized that by saying no to the little date, I was negotiating for a bigger one.

It's not that I was looking to go sailing—although it sure was nice—but I can promise you that the level of emotional intimacy we experienced by sitting on the bow of a boat watching the sun set behind the Statue of Liberty was way more intense than what we would have had watching Governor Schwarzenegger battle aliens (no offense, Ahnold). Now, was it easy for me to hedge my bet and say no to the movie? Hell no! I wanted to see that guy all the time. (Arthur, that is. Not Schwarzenegger.) But by learning how to play the waiting game, I became a woman worth upping the ante for. And the emotional bond.

Not Like *That*: Taking What You Can Get

I'm not always so smooth. A couple of months after Arthur, I met Quentin. Not only was he tall and handsome, but we had similar backgrounds. In fact, he grew up in a small town right near mine. Quentin's birthday was my mother's birthday, and we both loved Garth Brooks—I know, I know, scary, right? Anyway, too many coincidences can make your head spin. And so my head was spinning. After four weeks, I thought I was ready to buy the white dress and be done with it. Looking back, I can see that I missed some signs. Clear signs. Big ones. Like the off-ramp to the freeway. But I missed them. Because I thought it was love.

Sure, Quentin typically only asked me out on the weekdays. And sure, he had yet to introduce me to his friends. But he always seemed really busy . . . even though he was a television writer who, at that time, wasn't writing anything. But I ignored all those signs, and every time Quentin would call, my heart would leap, and my brain would lie. I kept saying yes to whatever was put in front of me: coffee at six P.M. on a Wednesday, dinner on a Thursday night, and even when he did ask me out to lunch on a Saturday, we ended up getting pizza. It was a very short date.

By Week Four, I was getting tired of it. He asked me out yet again for a Thursday, and I thought, enough. The buck stops here. I told him that I couldn't, that I was busy Thursday night. Point for me. But then I asked him if he could do Friday or Saturday night instead. Really, Amy? Basically, I was saying, "Any time will work because I don't have anything else going on other than waiting for you to ask me out on a proper date." Because sadly, at this point, I would have cancelled dinner with the president to get a Friday-night date, which means any semblance of control I had was long gone.

He paused on the other end of the line. And I waited. I was just about to concede further, offering my Sunday, too, when he said, "You know, I'm still dating other women."

I tried to make light of it, "Oh, well, I'm still dating other men." Lie, lie, lie. As if my "Let's do Friday night or Saturday night" offer wasn't a dead giveaway.

I was so busy rushing forward, waiting for his calls, that I had stopped dating other men by Week Two. And even if I was dating other men, you don't tell someone else that! This guy was being a jerk, and he was basically putting it in my face that he was dating other women. But using my own fake dates as a weapon didn't help. Instead, I just came off as an immature girl, singing, "I know you are and so am I!" What I should have said was "Trust me, I'm not sitting here waiting for you to make a marriage proposal because we've been out on a few dates." But that's not how I handled it.

"Oh, good," he continued. "Well, then you understand. I already have two dates set up this weekend."

It was Week Four and he had two dates set up over the weekend and I wasn't getting either? Some other girls had made it to the weekend and I was still stuck with Starbucks on a Tuesday. Though I might have had my head in the clouds for the last four weeks, I finally pulled the chute and came crashing back down to the ground. And from that point on, Quentin had no more dates with me.

Your Place or Mine

Up until now, you should not have stepped one little baby toe into his place (or him into yours). But if you're going to continue to play in the league, it's important to see where the other team sleeps. Going over to each other's places does not need to and shouldn't lead to heavier hook-ups. So if he invites you over after dinner, or even better, invites you over for dinner, say yes, and remember, you are not there to spend the night, you are there to get to know each other better . . . with your clothes on!

One of my good friends, Gina, had been following my

eight-week suggestions to the tee. She was so tired of not making it past Week Two that she said she would do whatever I told her to finally get somewhere with a man. And by somewhere, she meant anywhere but his bedroom. And therein lies the secret. *Do not go into his bedroom!* Yes, by Week Four, it is time for dinner at his place or dinner at yours. It's part of the emotional bonding to see how you live.

Nothing good is going to happen if you go into his bedroom. In fact, it is scientifically proven—at least by my data—that if you even sit on his bed you might as well take off all of your clothes right then and there. This is why living rooms rock. Stay in the living room. Keep it to the couch. Keep it safe. Keep it middle-school style. Do you remember what that is? It's called dry humping. At this point, no one's belt buckle should get undone. And avoid wearing dresses so that you are stuck with all or nothing. I know it's hard. I

DATING CSI

You can pretty much expect that the first few times you go over to his place (or he goes over to yours) you'll both be doing a little crime-scene investigating. And I don't mean searching the place with a black light. No, you'll be looking at how you both live. Is he messy or clean; are there pictures of his friends and family around? Take stock of what you find and expect that he will be doing the same when he comes to your place.

know that once you start feeling the chemistry, it becomes even more difficult, but this is the point where you decide whether you are going to bond physically or you're going to bond emotionally. Because at Week Four, you don't know each other well enough to do both.

As much as we wish we could multitask love, the truth is it's a lot more simple and straightforward than the rest of our lives. It demands that we take it one step at a time. We have to build the emotional intimacy first, and then we can focus on the physical intimacy. But if we try to do both at the same time, we will end up building neither. That's why you are laying the bricks of your relationship piece by piece. So you can have something strong, solid, and committed. Otherwise, if you try to slap it all together at once, it is only bound to fall apart.

Think of it like this: You are asking for a relationship and he is asking for sex. So if you give him what he wants, you risk not getting what you want.

If you haven't committed to liking each other enough to be exclusive, then do you like each other enough to have sex? I am not saying you will never get to do it, but if you wait just a few more weeks, you won't be doing the deed with some guy you've just begun to fall for, you'll be having sex with your boyfriend.

Don't be like my client Alina who made it to Week Four only to go to bed with her new man Jack. He said he would get in touch the next day. Well, he did. He texted her, "Have a good day."

What a shame, because at four weeks in, Alina and Jack were doing great. They had been going out to dinner and hitting golf balls off the Chelsea Piers. They even went to his best friend's birthday party, where Alina could hear him almost call her his girlfriend.

"She's my, um, my, she's my friend. My date. My date friend."

So freaking close. So when Jack invited Alina over for dinner, she was thrilled. She couldn't wait to see where and how he lived, and then when he added he was making his mother's special recipe for chicken cacciatore, she thought, "Has he told his mother about me, too?"

There were a lot of high hopes here. A lot of them. So when dinner was over and the wine was flowing and the Alicia Keys was playing, Alina forgot that they were still in Week Four. She went along when he insisted that they go lay down on what he advertised as the most comfortable bed in the world. And sure enough, there went her clothes.

She came in to meet with me on Friday once the denial began to wear off, and I could tell it had been a rough week.

She explained, "I'm too old to be going through this. You know, I used to sleep with men *on the first date.* You'd think that by a month they should be able to handle it."

For whatever reason, we think that dating works like dog years. That somehow, a month is this incredibly long period of time in which to get to know someone. It's not. But even more than that, when you are dating someone, you are negotiating a deal.

This is why Week Four is all about keeping firm to those physical boundaries. I can promise that if all a guy wants is sex, there is no better way to weed him out than not to give it to him.

---

intimacy *n.*: a close, familiar, and usually affectionate or personal relationship; what makes dating so delicious; not to be confused with sex.

Meet the Friends

So what should your dates look like by now? We've mentioned sailing, golfing, dinner at his place. Though the where, what, and when are all important, there is also another element that should be coming into play: who. I'm not saying you need to go to his family's Thanksgiving dinner, but you should start getting the sense that his friends have heard about you, and that it is time to meet them.

Hopefully, by this time, such an opportunity has shown up: the work party, the birthday dinner, the intramural softball game, or even just a double date with his already happily coupled friends. This is a two-part test. The first part is whether or not he's inviting you at all—test passed. And second is how his friends react. There is probably no more important time for you to be aware than at that meeting.

Are they excited to meet you? Or do they see a lot of women come through his life?

Date Like *This*: The Team Approach

Last year, one of my male clients Brandon decided it was time to introduce Megan, a girl he had been dating, to his friends. Before the meeting he wrote that he was nervous about such an introduction because his ex was also friends with his group. Never easy for the new girl.

> *From: Brandon*
> *Subject: Party*
>
> *Hey Amy—So things have been going really well with Megan. She is super awesome and, I don't know, I guess it's been a while since I really liked someone. I forgot how fun it can be. So . . . I have this birthday party to go to next week but all my ex's friends will be there. Not my ex—thank God! But we still have some mutual friends. I want to bring Megan so she can meet some of them but I also don't want it to be weird. What should I do?*

I wrote him back and explained that he should give Megan a heads-up beforehand, so that she didn't think his friends' awkwardness had anything to do with her. The issue was really about his ex-girlfriend. His concern was sweet, he wanted to protect her, but he also wanted to introduce her to his friends. I felt Megan deserved to know all of that.

I told him, "There is no better way to gain her confidence than to be honest with her. If you are open from the

Meeting each other's friends can be a big step forward—or backward. It's up to you to take the temperature, determining how his relationship with his friends reflects on him and you. Here are eight questions to ask yourself after you meet his friends:

1. How do his friends treat you?
2. How do they make you feel?
3. How does he behave around them?
4. How do they behave around him?
5. Do they bring up other women he has dated?
6. Do they bring up his ex-girlfriend(s)?
7. Do they act like he has talked about you before?
8. Do they seem happy to see him with you?

Because, I can promise you, how they act has nothing to do with what you say or what you wear or how the night goes. It has everything to do with their opinion of your guy, what he might have said about you thus far, and the women he has previously dated.

get-go, and head into the party like partners, not only will she respect you more, but it will give you both an opportunity to be there for each other."

Sure enough, Megan understood Brandon's concerns, and told him that his friends would just have to get over it. That night, they went there not as two people trying to figure each other out, but as a team. He told her the scoop on everyone at the party, and they had so much fun together that they forgot to pay attention to what everyone else thought. As they were leaving, one of Brandon's friends, and a close friend of his ex, told him that she was glad to see Brandon so happy.

Not Like *That*: Secret Lovers

So, let's do a little rewind back to Quentin, the television writer who was too busy dating other women to properly date me. The truth is if you feel like he is hiding you, he is probably hiding something. By Week Four, he should want to learn more about your life, and he should want to share his. With Quentin, neither of those was happening. And there is no worse feeling for your self-esteem than to feel like the girl on the side.

You have known him for four weeks. You have committed time, energy, and quite a bit of emotion, and you should not be treated like an a la carte item on the menu, but rather the main course.

We've talked about being a weekday girl (bad, bad), but you also don't want to become a lady of the night. If by Week Four he is only asking you to dinners or drinks, deny, deny, deny.

Do not agree to keep dating like that. You can say no. You can say that your nights are already booked. And if he still fails to ask you out during the day, you can say, "Sayonara!"

I have a good friend who was in this situation. She lives in New York and her would-be boyfriend lived in Connecticut so he would forgo weekend dates, telling her he was tired from commuting all week. Sure, they would go to dinner in the city after work. And he would take her out for romantic Friday nights, going to a Broadway show or the hottest club. He would even meet her for lunch during the workday. She felt like she was being courted in all the right ways. When she had him over for dinner at her place, they ate, made out, and then he told her that he needed to go home, but added, "Some day, I hope to stay the night."

Even with all of this romantic courting, she was annoyed that they never spent any weekend days together, so she mentioned that she had family in Connecticut that she would be visiting over Thanksgiving.

"Perhaps we could get lunch. Your town is right on my train route," she suggested.

She could hear him swallow hard. "Um, yeah, I've actually decided to head out of town that weekend."

She knew his family was also in Connecticut so she was confused . . . and suspicious. She had done some basic Googling on her man, but she decided to dig deeper. For $9.95, she got her answer. Mr. Secret Lover was actually some woman's not-so-secret husband.

Certainly, not every guy who fails to ask you out on a Sunday during the day is married, but if you are seeing such signs, do not let your guard down. Do any advanced research you need to do, and if it's still taking him some time, refuse to see him at night, nudging him oh-so subtly in the right direction.

Date Like *This*: Letting Down Your Guard

So let's say you're not dealing with Mr. Mysterious. Let's say your guy is asking you out for weekends, weekdays, brunches, lunches, and plans with his friends. This is feeling really good and all of his actions are supporting that feeling. Let's say you're sitting on a park bench lost in conversation, and you're deciding whether to share with him that your mother is manic-depressive, or that you once had an eating disorder. If everything else is going well, now is your time to let down that guard we have spent the last four weeks carefully crafting.

By letting your guard down you are opening up the conversation for him to do the same.

My client Serena had been dating Paul for four weeks when she decided she wanted to take it to the next emotional level. If you remember, Paul was the guy who got thrown off by Leslie, who unfortunately sent that text about the Jets and was quickly tossed into the "buddy" category. After that first experience, he was pleased to be dating the lady-like Serena. A former ballerina and now a choreographer, Serena did not have the easiest childhood. She had grown up on the stage and with that, all the trappings of a dancer's life: extreme stress, unhealthy eating habits, and a stunted childhood.

When Serena was seventeen, she checked herself into a mental inpatient program. She wrote me:

From: Serena
Subject: Paul

Hey Amy,
Hope you're doing well. I just wanted to give you an update on Paul and me. Things have been going great between us and I feel like we've both been getting more intimate (don't worry, I've been keeping it PG)! But I also don't know what too intimate means. I keep feeling like I want to tell him about what my childhood was like.

Doing ballet and all. And I wasn't sure how much I should tell. I guess I'm just afraid I'm going to give TMI. But then I also feel like I am really beginning to trust him and isn't that how you build trust? So I guess I'm just feeling a little stuck. . . . Other than that, it's been really great. Like really great. So wild!

S

Serena had learned so much from her past, becoming a different and much healthier person because of it; she wanted to share that with the man who was becoming a more serious part of her life. I told her not to make a big deal about it, but if there was an opportunity to bring up her past casually, it could lead to a real breakthrough in intimacy.

Sure enough, that weekend Paul and Serena went to see a ballet she had choreographed. Afterward, they talked about her time on the stage, and some of her emotional difficulties in the aftermath. Serena talked about how she works to help other dancers manage the emotional stress, particularly young people. Paul asked her if she would like to do that for a living, and the conversation soon changed to how Paul was once a Big Brother and how helping kids has always meant so much to him. He told her that since he was an only child, he always felt a little isolated, and that helping others finally made him feel like he belonged.

Afterward, I spoke with Serena, and she told me, "I think the most important thing that came out of talking about my past is that it actually became a conversation about what was important to both of us. Not only did Paul sympathize, he also saw it the same way I did—as part of who I am and who I hope to be."

Clearly, not everyone is in a place to tell their deep, dark secrets by Week Four, but if you feel so close that you want to have sex with this person, perhaps you need to ask yourself if you are close enough to first let down your emotional guard.

Not Like *That*: One-Dimension Debbie

So, I know up until this point, you've been playing it cool. You didn't unload all of your secrets on the first date. You've learned to hold those cards close to your chest and keep the conversation light. All of that works really well . . . at first. But as you continue to get to know someone, the stakes get higher, and so should your level of trust and emotional intimacy. This is not about breaking down about your first marriage, or asking him to hold you while you cry. It's about showing him that there is more to you than meets the eye.

So, by Week Four you should be getting a lot more comfortable. You should feel that you are dating a man you can open up to, that you can trust and who will respect your experiences and empathize with whatever you have been through. If you're not getting that feeling, raise a flag.

If you are with a guy who wants to make this relationship serious, he will want to start talking about more serious

INTIMACY-R-US

Let's take a look at how the intimacy is stacking up:

1. Does he want to talk about more serious things, such as his family, his job, even his political beliefs?
2. Does he just like to joke around—keeping things light and superficial?
3. When you mention your family or childhood, does he engage or change the subject?
4. Do you feel like you can be yourself around him or that you have to pretend?
5. Is your conversation natural and easy, or do you feel like you're searching for something to say?
6. Does he make you laugh and does he laugh at your jokes?
7. Does he ask deeper questions about your life; is he beginning to delve a little deeper into who you are?
8. When you do try to talk about something serious, does he listen and respond?

topics. And if you want to make the relationship more serious, you need to be sure that he is someone who you feel comfortable having such conversations with. If not, you might want to pull that guard back up and see if this is really someone you can trust.

Date Like *This*: Feeling the Pink Cloud

I've said it before and I am going to say it again: By now you better be having fun. And I don't mean fun as in "I got a pedicure today" fun—I mean, silly, lighthearted, "the hills are alive with the sound of music" fun. I recently had a client who felt that after four weeks of going out with Michael, dating was still a chore. Francesca had been divorced for two years when she came to me. She had just opened a new boutique and was ready to start dating again. As she told me in our first meeting, "I feel like I've been dead inside for years. I want to live!"

So when her first few dates with Michael went well, I had high hopes that she would start a new relationship alongside her career. She was taking it slow, and at first, she thought that was why she wasn't getting any early romance jitters. This was her first time back in the dating pool, and she had no intention of jumping right into the deep end. But after a month of seeing Michael, she was still in the wading pond.

From: Francesca
Subject: Hmm . . .

So, missy, I'm not sure if I should be writing this already, but I feel like I need your advice. As you know, Michael and I have been dating for almost a month and it's been going well enough, but I still feel something is missing. As you probably remember this was my fear from the start, but the dates have continued . . . and believe me he is a great dater. We've done amazing things. We even went to the Hamptons for lunch one day! I just feel . . . bored. I know what I normally feel like when I am falling for someone and it just isn't happening. I'm bummed and I keep saying give it one more chance, but is that fair? I feel like I am leading him on, and that I should be feeling a little something by now.

I agreed. If by Week Four, you are not feeling at least a little thump in your heart, you need to look at that and figure out why. Is it you? Is it him? This isn't an excuse to run, but rather to see what's leaving you blah.

If you're not feeling it, don't force it. Know that, sometimes, chemistry and personality and that special dose of magic don't always come just because we want them to.

Francesca later wrote me, "I was in a loveless marriage for ten years. I don't want to do that again. Neither to me nor to someone else. I would rather meet the right one who sweeps me off my feet than feel like I've settled just because I don't want to be alone."

Not Like *That*: Don't Let Your Feet off the Ground

I know most women were raised to believe in fairy tales. That damn Cinderella and that insipid Snow White and her dwarves taught us from an early age that all we had to do was sing a few songs and sweep the kitchen floor, and voilà, Prince Charming would appear. And so we grow up and we meet a man and within a few weeks, we are humming to the birds outside.

---

fairy tale *n.*: a story told to amuse children; an interesting but highly implausible story, often told as an excuse; the reason women kiss far too many frogs.

We are so susceptible to that pink cloud, you'd think we lived in the sky. For so many of us, romance sends us up in the air like a balloon. But if you've ever seen what a balloon looks like when it finally makes its way back down to the earth, well, that's often what it looks like when we are brought back down, too. And believe me, I know. Often, way too often, you meet someone and just because they "seem" perfect or do "all the right things," you are off to the races. And you leave behind the reins.

You forget to pay attention to what he is doing, and miss the signs. So here we are in our fourth week. We are letting down our guard. We are getting a little (again, a little) more physical, and we are feeling that hormonal bliss called mutual attraction.

And this is when you need to hold back your horse, and really pay attention—not only to how he is treating you but also how you are feeling about him. You need to first ask yourself: Are you ready for emotional intimacy? Do you want it with this person? Are you watching out for any red flags, and are you throwing down any yourself? I know that for so long, I was just trying to get to Week Four, which seemed like a feat in itself. By the time I was there, I had lost sight of the larger picture—meeting, getting to know, and building a relationship with someone I liked . . . and who liked me back. So as much as you should be having the time of your life, you have to be able to stop yourself and make sure it's because of the person you are with, and not just because you are finally with a person.

FUN FACT: Men aren't the only ones who get confused. Women can have their own versions of Dating ADD. Don't mistake your own lust for love. Don't assume you want the relationship to move forward just because you want a relationship.

Date Like *This*: Becoming Friends

After her experience with Michael, Francesca, the divorcée starting a new boutique and a new life, continued to be matched up. Sadly, one after the next, there were no sparks. Sometimes it was on her part, and sometimes it was on the part of the guy. I told her not to get disappointed. Love wasn't about the no's. Love was all about finding your one big YES. She was getting frustrated but she stuck it out. She told me that she was trying to view dating like she viewed tennis. It wasn't always about winning the match, but about having fun trying. Good for you, Francesca!

And that was the attitude she had when I sent her on her first date with Peter. So by Week Four, when I got an e-mail from Peter telling me why Francesca was different, I was elated.

From: Peter
Subject: Francesca

All right, sorry I haven't written you. I've just been really busy between work and, well, Francesca. We've been spending more and more time together, and for the first time in a long time I feel like I am not just dating a woman, I am dating a friend. It's just so comfortable to be with her. Not only is she beautiful, she's so caring and kind and, okay, I'll stop there. Anyway, I'll keep you posted but I was thinking about inviting her to go skiing over Halloween. I think I've always had to second-guess myself, but with Francesca it just feels right.

Peter

Well, Peter hit that one on the head. Though you probably aren't going to be besties at this point, you should feel that the potential is there. He should be opening up to you about his bad day at work, and should be offering kind advice when you come to him with yours. He should bring you soup to help you get over a cold, and you should make him tea to help. I'm not saying that all this has to happen to prove that you're good friends, but this is how good friends behave.

Not Like *That*: Staying Buddies

Don't be a buddy. Just as I warned in Week One, a buddy is a terrible fate. Unfortunately, as time goes on and women get more comfortable, they make the same mistakes and risk falling into the buddy role that they were so careful to avoid in those early days.

Guys drink pitchers of beer with their buddies. They complain about women with their buddies. They could care less about going out of their way to impress a buddy. You started as a lady, so you should continue being one.

I hate that I even have to say this, but being a lady means: no sex, no farting, no burping, no dirty jokes, no heavy drinking, no asking him out, and no going out on the same day that he asked.

Buddies call each other up for last-minute chill time. Friends set plans. This is the difference between a relationship moving forward or fizzling out. Recently, one of my friends called me because she had just gotten home from another date with her new guy. They both realized early on that they loved the same football team, the Patriots. And if you know any Pats fans, they're pretty crazy about their team. Marisa was excited to meet someone with whom she could watch games, drink beer, and yell at the television. And she thought that Jim would feel the same way.

At first, their dates took place in restaurants around town, but as they started watching more games together, the dates moved to sports bars. She went from shrimp cocktail to popcorn shrimp and chicken wings. Marisa said, sighing, "I don't get it. He tells me how much fun he has with me, but I feel like we're going in the other direction. At first, we were having these passionate kisses, and tonight it was barely a peck on the lips."

She was lucky it wasn't a slap on the butt. Because as much as it is totally cool to like football, you need to be more than that to a guy. You need to be a woman who likes the Pats, not a Pats fan who happens to be a woman. Later down the line, you can incorporate your love of football into the relationship, but early on, if there are any signs that you could fall into buddy territory, stay out. Don't go to the sports bar. Don't join him for his guys' night watching baseball. Keep yourself strictly in the girl's club until you are actually in a relationship. That way there will be no confusion. That doesn't mean you need to lie about your love of sports and beer, just don't become his Saturday afternoon cheering buddy.

If you think of him for that first phone call when something happens—whether good or bad—and he's doing the same with you, then you can be sure you are creating a firm and solid friendship for whatever comes next.

WEEK FOUR: CHOOSE YOUR OWN RELATIONSHIP

Week Four is one of the most challenging. You are halfway there, and likewise, you should feel at least half of something serious by now. Yes, there is a part of you floating on a cloud, but you also haven't forgotten that you're dating differently this time. Keep one hot eye on the prize, and one cool eye on how that prize is treating you. In order to establish more emotional intimacy, stay away from getting too physical, while slowly letting down some of your guard. Because here's the deal: If you can hold out on having sex for just a while longer (or doing *anything* below the belt for that matter), not only will you keep yourself from falling into the deep postsex love that women have a tendency to trip up on (blame it on the hormones), but you will also find yourself in a real relationship *before* you have sex.

This is the time when you lay the cement of friendship, which will become the foundation of your relationship. There is no room for buddies. If you are serious about finding a boyfriend, now more than ever you need to watch your behaviors (and his) to set yourself up for the wonderful feeling of falling in love. It is up to you. You hold the reins. How you handle them in this week will determine what happens in the next one.

Eight Steps to Everlasting

1. Let him make the call. Don't call him.
2. You should be seeing each other more than before, but you should also have time in between.
3. If he makes you the weekday girl or a lady of the night, use your influence to change the situation. If he doesn't respond, cut him loose.
4. If you participate in a hobby or activity, don't alter that schedule.
5. Set aside time every weekend for friends or even for just some downtime for yourself.
6. Remember, you are negotiating a deal. You're asking for a relationship. He's asking for sex. The goal is to hold off on the sex until you get the relationship.
7. Don't let your guard down. If you're feeling suspicious, don't live in denial. Do your research and make sure the guy you're dating is who he says he is.
8. Check in with your emotions—is this someone you want to be with?

Week Five

You Put One Foot In, You Keep One Foot Out

Are We "Exclusive"?

Week Five always takes me back to the fifth grade, when I learned one of my first major lessons in dating: Don't jump ahead. I had been crushing on Scott all summer. A green-eyed soccer player, he happened to be the tallest kid in our grade (yes, my infatuation with height came early), and with his wispy hair and mischievous smile, he basically had me melting by the time we were back at school. Ah, the torture of young love. To my absolute thrill, just one week later Scott made the usual fifth-grade overtures and, suddenly, we were "seeing each other." I was the luckiest girl at my New Jersey elementary school.

There is no better way to sabotage the relationship than to put your guy on the spot.

Once we started holding hands, I thought of us as "official," even though Scott hadn't "officially" asked me out. One Friday, on our school bus, I passed him a note that said, "I really like you. Do you like me?" It seemed like the right thing to do. Well, that weekend we ended up at a birthday party together and people started slow dancing. Just as Phil Collins came on (I know, I know—"A Groovy Kind of Love" still gets me), I watched him separate from his group of friends and head my way. This was it. He was going to ask me to dance and make our status official. But he didn't. He turned to my best friend, who was standing next to me, and asked her to dance instead. Like it was nothing.

I can still feel the dagger in my stomach, and I can still recall the puffy eyes and broken heart that came after that terrible party. How could this happen to me? It wasn't fair. Why did he walk by me? What did I do wrong?

You know. Don't you?

I told him I liked him. And I asked him if he liked me.

That may have happened in the fifth grade, but I'm betting it's happened to each and every one of us. More than once. Still.

Keep Calm and Date On

It's hard to maneuver through our grown-up relationships. We're vulnerable. We're excited. We're scared. We're hopeful.

And we feel like we're on shaky ground, particularly when we hit Week Five and are waiting for the "exclusivity" conversation. We start worrying that he doesn't like us—maybe he likes someone else!—and we want to push for confirmation. We want to pass that note.

Here's the thing: the rules haven't changed since fifth grade. There is no better way to sabotage the relationship than to put your guy on the spot. Week Five is just as tricky for the guy as it is for you. He's feeling things, nice things, things that make him want to call you his girlfriend and stop seeing other people. But that's scary for him. Sure, he might want a girlfriend in theory but as he realizes he is actually getting one, he might get nervous.

Nervous? You need to remain calm and know that if you keep holding the reins, you can ride this one out.

Be careful not to damage the relationship with any last-minute negativity. Last year, my friend Jenny had been dating this guy Max for over a month. Jenny is a writer in Chicago and had been single almost as long as I have at this point. Needless to say, she was thrilled about Max. Things had been going great, but the fact that Max hadn't asked her to be "his girlfriend" yet started to get her really freaked out. She started obsessing about everything he said and did. She would call friends in the middle of the night (that was fun!) with some harebrained idea about how he was going to dump her the next day. And when they would be out with each other, she would act nervous, more nervous than she had been in the beginning.

The sad part was that things were actually going really well. Max had met her friends and they had gone out a couple of times with his. They had made dinner at his place one night and he totally respected her when she went home after. They were falling for each other. And then Jenny became, for lack of a better word, a moron.

When they would go out, if Max even looked at the waitress a second too long, she would find herself wondering whether he thought the waitress was prettier. If he were five minutes late to meet her, she would convince herself that he wasn't interested. And though she wouldn't act on these crazy ideas, the mind is a powerful thing. Our thoughts carry a certain energy with them, and by the end of Jenny and Max's fifth week of dating, she was carrying a really unattractive, nervous, and pretty darn crazy energy.

When Max began distancing himself, she didn't know what to do. She sent him seven texts in a row. She asked him out for Friday night before he even had the chance to ask, and then in a last-ditch effort to save things (okay, so she was totally breaking the rules here), she slept with him. The sad part is had Jenny focused on all the good things happening in the relationship and not her fears, it might have worked out. She wasn't surprised when Max broke up with her. She had decided it was coming long before he had.

Date Like *This*: Take the Temperature

Again, you ask? Yes, again. You see, the biggest issue in dating is vagueness. We don't know what's happening so we make stuff up to fill in the missing parts. The old question of "does he or doesn't he" pulls at us, and the only real solution is to have some clarity—or we start feeling crazy fast. Like me in fifth grade, we get so swept up in what we think is "about to be" that we stop paying attention to "what actually is." We start sugarcoating everything, even the stuff that doesn't make sense. Because in Week Five, not only are you both beginning to let your guard down, you are also beginning to show your true colors.

So look at Week Five as the opportunity it is.

This isn't just about whether he's into you. Ask yourself this: Is he someone I should be into? Is he treating me the way I deserve to be treated?

Here's why we're taking out that thermometer again: we need to be aware of what may be signs of problems ahead. It's funny the things that we can immediately spot in others' relationships, but we fail to see for ourselves. Those darn feelings. They always get in the way, don't they?

My friend Natalie, a boisterous little brunette with the personality of a firecracker, was dating a local radio DJ, Cole, for a little over a month when she began to see some not-so-great signs. Cole would always comment if he thought her skirt was too short, and would give people looks if he thought they were looking in her direction. He was constantly asking her, "Who are you texting?" or "Who were you just on the phone with?" And though he was low-key about it, he seemed to be put off by the fact that she had two very close guy friends. One who was *gay,* mind you, and the other who was married!

Though Nat thought all these things were a little weird, everything else about Cole seemed so great that she downplayed it. One night they were at their favorite dive bar watching Sunday football when Cole got up to use the bathroom. Just a few minutes later, someone came over to the table and approached Natalie, who happens to be a social butterfly. As it turned out, the guy was actually dating one of Natalie's friends and recognized her from a party they had both been to the weekend before. Sorta cool, right? The conversation was brief and it seemed like the man in question was trying to score points with his own new girl by saying hi to one of her friends. He even brought up the fact he was taking out his lady that next night. Nat was impressed . . . until Cole walked up. He was jealous and quickly started an argument at the table, threatening her friend's new boyfriend. The entire way back to his apartment, Cole accused Nat of picking up guys behind his back. And please don't think for a moment that this means, "Gee, he must really like me, look at how protective he's being." He doesn't and he isn't. Thankfully, that was a night Natalie couldn't ignore, and she put an end to it right there.

TAKE THE TEMPERATURE ON HIS PERSONALITY

In your heart of hearts, are you listening to your instincts or making excuses?

The big lesson here? Don't ignore the small stuff until it's too late.

Not Like *That*: Excuses, Excuses

At this point, you're probably awash in hormones. Even without sleeping with him, your estrogen, serotonin, and dopamine levels are at an all-time high. And your voice of reason has lost its reason, telling you that whatever man you are dating would make the perfect boyfriend if only he would ask. You are so focused on *getting* the guy, you are most likely willing to let some other things slide. Stop that now. This is not the time for excuses. This is the time for cold hard facts.

If you are in your fifth week, and the man in question is backing off, or is acting different, then you need to focus on that, and not on what you think might be.

This is not about dating someone for his potential; this is about dating someone based on who he is right now and how he's treating you.

Learn to *listen* to what he's telling you. And not just with his words. He is telling you as much, if not more, by his actions. If it's been five weeks and he is treating you like you're in Week Two, it's no coincidence. Chances are he doesn't like you *that much,* so let's stop the story, shall we? I know that might be painful. And you're probably thinking, "I totally agree, Amy. But you see, my guy is different. He's just suuuuper busy at the moment and that's why he hasn't called." No, it isn't. Yes, I am talking to *you.* (And part of you, the honest part, *knows* it.)

Last year, two of my clients had been going out for almost six full weeks when I got the e-mail that all was not well. Tamara was in international sales for a cosmetics company, and Dillon, a tall and handsome redhead, was in marketing for a financial firm. Both had busy work schedules, but for the first few weeks they had managed to always make time to see each other. They agreed that they both finally wanted to make dating a priority. Fantastic! Time to release the reins, right? No. Because, lo and behold, a month rolled around and suddenly Dillon's job kept getting in the way. Tamara wrote me:

From: Tamara
Subject: Dillon

So, I just got back from yet another great date with Dillon. And I guess I would be excited about it except that we hadn't seen each other in over a week, and I think the only reason we did tonight was because he texted me as I was leaving the office and I agreed to meet up for dinner. I know he has a really busy job but it just feels like something's changed. We were seeing each other two to three times a week at first and now it's like, hello? Where'd you go? I guess I wouldn't feel so weird if he seemed to think this was a temporary thing, but I don't know if it makes sense for me to date a guy who works all the time. Am I jumping the gun here? I guess I'm just surprised it's not going the way I expected it to at this point. Ugh. Hate this. I'm sorta confused. Help?

I told Tamara to give it another week or two to see if his schedule changed, but then, a mere two days later, I received an e-mail from Dillon saying that he didn't think it was going anywhere with Tamara, and he asked if I might have some other matches for him. I was blown away, and told him as much, saying, "Dillon, I can't ethically set you up with someone else until you have told Tamara that you are not interested. People need to be adult enough to be honest with each other. You don't have to be perfect or like someone you aren't into, but you do have to be upfront with them. Also, in the future, please do not use your work as an excuse with women. If you decide that you want to see someone else, please let me or them know so that they are not misled."

Don't be so focused on *getting* the guy that you let things slide. Ask yourself this: Is he *worth* getting?

I was really annoyed with Dillon, even though he did end up agreeing with me and apologizing for being a numbskull. (His word.) He told me that he didn't intend to lead Tamara on. In fact, he thought he was telling her the truth. Because he did like her, just not as much as she thought, or as much as she liked him.

There wasn't anything wrong with Dillon wanting to see other women or deciding that Tamara was not for him, but

EIGHT LITTLE THINGS THAT MEAN A LOT

Does he:

1. seem distracted when he's with you?
2. frequently reschedule your dates?
3. take longer than twenty-four hours to return your calls?
4. pay a lot of attention to his phone—texting and checking e-mails when you're together?
5. have trouble introducing you? ("This is Laura, she's my, um . . .")
6. check out other women when he's with you?
7. use work as an excuse not to see you?
8. consistently try to get you to go back to his place?

Do you know what time it is? Time to move on!

he was avoiding the situation by using work as his excuse, which meant that Tamara was also making it an excuse. Since you probably aren't going to have a middleman like me to help you through, do not make up stories to justify his behaviors. It's your job to be your own matchmaker, and to see when the signs are pointing in the wrong direction. Look for the flashing red lights of someone with Dating ADD or worse, someone who is jealous, possessive, or even just plain mean. If they are any of the above, get out before you get hurt. Refer back to this chapter as many times as needed, using it to help keep your head clear. If you can recognize the signs, you can negotiate your way out of any relationship that does not feel right. There is a time to wait things out, a time to hold the reins, and a time when you need to make the smart decision and amputate. Learn the difference.

Date Like *This*: Keep Up Your Profile

And by this, I mean your dating profile. Do *not* start dating exclusively until you are in an exclusive relationship. If you get a friendly invite to meet someone new for a drink after work, even if you only sort of like the other guy, go! If you are online, keep meeting men and going out for coffee. If a friend asks to set you up, you can say that you're seeing someone but that it's not exclusive. There's no better way to keep one foot out than to be out there dating. This is not the time to hunker down in the fantasy relationship you are creating.

This is the time to be meeting new people and also seeing how your guy stacks up.

I know this is hard. Once we meet someone we like, going out on other dates can feel depressing. We think there is no way we're going to meet another guy who would measure up, dismissing anyone else before we've even had the chance to meet them. Don't look at these dates as consolation for not being exclusive, look at them as competition for your guy. You're not dating just to waste time waiting around for him; you're dating because you are an attractive, interesting woman who men want to meet. And that confidence, my friend, will help you to be open without fear, giving you the freedom to have *fun* dating.

A few years back, right as my ex Adrian and I were about to become exclusive, I started sending myself out on dates rather than focus all my attention on him. It worked! I would go out with men who I didn't necessarily think I would like, but I still gave them a chance. Now, does that mean I was going out with these guys just to use them? No. I kept an open mind when I went out with them. I recognized that I wasn't with Adrian yet, so why not get back into the dating scene and make sure that Adrian was right for me . . . and that someone else wasn't? And by going out with other men, I stopped obsessing over Adrian. I was too busy to lose the reins, and the more control I felt over the situation, the firmer my grip became.

The dates not only assured me that I wanted to be with Adrian, they also showed me why Adrian should want to be with me. These other men would open doors, compliment me, do what they could to woo me, and then when I would go back out with Adrian, I'd feel like a million bucks. I wouldn't think about how much better he was than my other dates, I would think how lucky he was to be dating me!

Going out with other men helped me to value myself. I knew I deserved someone who wanted to woo me, and by not settling for less, I somehow communicated that to Adrian. (Influence, my friend!) And it worked. Adrian wooed me right into a long-term relationship. For once, I followed my own rules, and I learned just how much better dating could be.

Not Like *That*: Stop Waiting by the Phone

Get out there. Be social. And for goodness sake, don't turn down casual dates with other men. You should not be so available that he can text you whenever he wants and know he's going to get a date. You don't want to be making up other obligations, pretending you've got things going on when you don't. (He'll probably know it and, besides, that's not who you are.) So go out and get yourself busy.

FUN FACT: An active woman who needs advance notice will be regarded as a commitment, not an afterthought. And isn't commitment what you're looking for?

I had a client who kept forgetting about this. Tanya was the child psychologist who got annoyed when the guy she was dating refused to open up. She had continued along in the relationship with Lawrence despite his high walls, but this only made Tanya more nervous . . . and needy. Because Lawrence wasn't giving her what she required emotionally, Tanya began to seek it from him physically. And though she was still managing to stave off sex, every time Lawrence would call, Tanya would say yes. But then Lawrence started calling less and less. Tanya wrote me one morning:

From: Tanya
Subject: Lawrence Again

Oh, Amy. I don't know what to do. I like Lawrence so much and we're such a perfect match but lately I feel like he is only pulling away more. After our last talk, I started trying to hold my horses or the reins or whatever, but then it just felt like I wasn't getting to see him as much as I wanted. So I figured, forget it. When he asks me out, I'll go out with him. I mean, if it's meant to be, why play hard to get? But now he's only been calling me once a week. And the last time we hung out, he really seemed more interested in getting back to my place than doing anything else. I am so confused. What am I doing wrong? And, yes, I know you're going to tell me!

XO,
Tanya

AVOIDING THE "MEANT TO BE" TRAP

There's no such thing as "meant to be." I'm not saying we are going to fall in love with every man we meet or that if you follow the rules set out in this book you will find romance in the world. But if you meet someone you like, it's not fate's job to make it work and it's not fate's fault if it doesn't.

So, about that "meant to be" stuff? We don't know if something is meant to be or if we're not doing our best to make it that way. Let's be honest—isn't "not meant to be" the name we give to our mistakes? It's like baking a cake. If you don't add the right ingredients, or if you bake it at the wrong temperature or for twice as long, then yeah, sure, that cake wasn't meant to be. But if you do everything according to the directions, then chances are things are going to turn out a lot better.

By giving in to the "meant to be" trap, you are giving up your power. And not just in the fledgling relationship that you're trying to build with one guy, but in your whole dating life. "Meant to be" assumes that someone (him?) or something else (fate?) is guiding your love life. Why would you relinquish your power like that? Why should you?

I had to break it to Tanya. There was nothing about Lawrence's behavior that said he was interested, and the fact that she was so willing to let herself be treated like second place wasn't going to help.

Sometimes, a man will pull away after a few weeks because he is warming up to the fact that he likes you. He's getting used to the idea. It's like sticking a foot into cold pool water. You might pull it out at first, but then slowly, you'll inch your way back in. Guys can be the same way when it comes to romance. So it's your job to stay cool, stay patient, and decipher whether this is someone who is just getting a little case of cold feet, or someone who has no intention of going swimming.

I reminded Tanya of this fact. I also reminded her how amazing she is, how our job is to learn and move forward. So, dear friends, don't wait by the phone and don't shrug off these suggestions. Follow them, and you will never have to ask yourself again, "What am I doing wrong?"

Hope Floats

A lot of women get scared in Week Five thinking that x, y, and z should have happened already, and if it hasn't, they start losing it. I have gotten calls from male clients saying, "She started texting me after ten P.M.—I was already asleep," or "I woke up in the morning to three missed calls." They'll tell me how women accuse them of seeing someone else, or not being interested, when they clearly are. And they'll share with me just how much all of this behavior freaks them out.

Acting crazy is no way to secure a man. Just as you don't need to make any excuses for his bad behavior, you also don't need to lose sight of the good stuff. If he asks you out in advance, if you are doing fun things on the weekends and getting to know each other, if you have hung out with his friends and he with yours, these are all wonderfully positive things that you should be excited about.

Often I will suggest to women to start writing down a list of things that are going well. What are the good things happening in your relationship and how is he making you feel? So, let's look at that. If you want to write down the eight most exciting parts of your relationship, you can use it for reference whenever you get scared. Sometimes, we need to list the cold hard facts in order to stay out of the crazy, estrogen-filled brain.

---

freak-out *n.*: senseless; impractical; totally unsound spaz attack because your relationship is not proceeding exactly as planned.

Recently, I had a friend try this. Tessa had been dating her new guy for about a month when she began to get worried. Everything was going great, but she had what we call "a sudden freak-out," which if left untreated will turn into freaking him out. But instead, she made her list and whenever she would get worried she would look back at it and remember why the good parts of the relationship were making it worth the risk. Here is what she wrote:

1. Robert calls me every day.
2. He brought me flowers on our last date.
3. He makes me laugh.
4. He cares about his family and I feel comfortable talking about mine.
5. Robert *loves* to travel.
6. He doesn't like it when people are rude and is always so nice.
7. He is a *great* kisser.
8. I feel like we could talk forever.

There are no guarantees in love, but if we remember why we're taking the plunge, it might feel a little less scary when we jump.

Date Like *This*: Dodgeball

Remember dodgeball, the game where people would throw colored balls at your head and it was your job not to get hit? Well, that's basically what you're doing on the topic of sex right now. Dodge, dodge, dodge. If he does come out and ask whether or not you're interested in having sex with him, stay general about it. You can say something to the effect of "I guess I'm still getting to know you. And I really like you, don't get me wrong, but I just want to wait till I'm with someone before I get that intimate."

How's that for big-girl stuff? How's that for power? Look, when you're in your early twenties having fun, maybe it's okay to forgo the relationship and go for the sex. But if you actually want a grown-up relationship, maybe one that will lead to marriage and kids, then you need to act like a grown-up.

A grown-up makes her own decisions, sets her own boundaries, and isn't afraid to say, "I want to wait until I'm with someone before I have sex with them."

If you need to look in the mirror and repeat those words to yourself twenty times each day, then I suggest you do it. This isn't about issuing ultimatums, which is why you should keep it general. Don't say "Until you and I are exclusive, I don't want to have sex." That just adds undue pressure, not to mention, it sounds a little threatening. This isn't about him; this is about you. This is about the standards that you set in *all* relationships.

Still think this sounds like the 1950s? Don't worry—it's not *that* bad.

You can make out. You can do anything you want, in fact, as long as everyone's zippers stay zipped, and your pants stay on. Do not give in to the puppy-dog eyes and the whispered sweet nothings enticing you to do more. If you have to stay out of his apartment to keep yourself safe, stay out. Pull back a little. And if he asks why, just tell him that you want to make sure you're not "rushing into anything." Again, you don't need to threaten or allude to exclusivity, you just need to stick to your guns, even as he is trying to bring out his.

If he wants you to share your exclusivity with him then

he better be ready to make it exclusive. We can pretend all we want that sex is a casual act, and if that's all you want it to be, then fine. But if you want to be having sex with your future life partner and father of your children, then you better stop thinking of it as casual. And so should he.

Not Like *That*: Giving In Is Giving Up

Have you ever had a friend who has trained for the marathon? Marathon runners are committed to slowly building up their miles—for months. They start with three miles, and then five, and then eight, twelve, twenty. They get themselves to the place where on race day they can confidently run the twenty-six miles that they have been preparing for. You would be hard-pressed to see them running the course and then give up at mile twenty-three. That's just not going to happen. They've worked too hard and for too long to stop in the final stretch.

But if you have sex now, that is exactly what you'll be doing. You'll be giving up on the last miles, when—had you only made it a couple of more weeks—you would have crossed the finish line into a real relationship. Because here is what you have been doing over the last five weeks: You have slowly been building the foundation of exclusivity. Building up from the first early dates, into spending more time together, getting to know each other on a more intimate level, meeting each other's friends, and deciding whether this is something you really want. And if you have done all of that while still managing to hold the reins and keep your pants on, why stop now?

Oh, that's right—because you are falling for him and you are making excuses. That is the only reason. And it's a pretty understandable one. But I have watched as way too many women (um, hello, me) assume they are in an exclusive relationship and then find themselves heartbroken when they have sex too soon. There is a reason we keep talking about this, ladies. Because it is one of the most important decisions you can make, and at this point, it is the most common act of sabotage that women run into in the last few miles of courtship. Just ask Michael, a network sales executive, who had been dating Melanie, a lawyer and fellow client, for five weeks. Though they had both been seeing other people, the relationship had continued to get more intense until Melanie decided they were exclusive before Michael did. They spent the weekend together, and as I later found out, had sex for most of it. He wrote me after:

From: Michael
Subject: Melanie

Hey Amy,
Hope you've been well. I know you wrote me a few weeks ago for an update with Melanie. Sorry I'm just getting back to you. I guess no news was good news because things had been going great but then we spent last

weekend together and I began to realize that I think Melanie was feeling this a little more than I am. I invited her over for dinner on Friday night but we'll see . . . Not sure this is going anywhere.

M.

I wrote Melanie immediately to see where she stood with everything and this was her response:

From: Melanie
Subject: Michael

Hey Amy,
Thanks for checking in on me! Things are going great. I spent last weekend at Michael's and it was amazing. I mean he didn't say that we're "exclusive" yet, but I don't think he needs to. Last weekend we clearly felt like a couple. He said he was really busy this week but we're having dinner at his place on Friday. I am not sure if I should bring up the talk but I kind of feel like he will. Thank you so much for bringing us together!

And that's when my job gets really hard. I asked Michael to please be honest with Melanie or I would be forced to. He did see her again that Friday night, and slept with her again, but the following week he ended things.

Sleeping with a man does not make it exclusive. If so, we would all be married by now.

Like any agreement, you need to have the terms clearly outlined before you agree to them. And by this point, haven't you done enough hard work to deserve that? This isn't about holding out for the sake of holding out. You are not playing a game. This is about holding out so that you are able to establish intimacy and trust. This is about holding out so that you get to know each other better and you are *both* sure you want to be with each other. This is about holding out for the relationship that could soon be yours.

Date Like *This*: Que Sera, Sera

When I received the following e-mail from my client Melissa, I could only think, "Hurray! Hurray!" If you remember, Melissa started as a complainer, then on her next match-up, invited her date Trent over for dinner on the third date. Well, finally, Melissa was progressing (this is why I don't give up on clients). Sometimes, all we need is a little guidance to finally learn how to be successful in love. Melissa had been seeing a new client of mine George for almost six weeks. She had really worked on staying positive, staying hopeful, and setting the pace. Though she had been to dinner twice at George's she had been keeping her cool, and also her confidence. She didn't stay the night. She remained busy enough in her own life to be able to be selective in saying yes to George's invites.

Even as the pressure began, she held on to her reins. She felt like she was really getting to know George. He had even asked if she would be interested in meeting his children from his first marriage, and she had gently agreed, offering, "As long as you are comfortable with it." A few days later, she wrote me, explaining how by using my suggestions, she was feeling confident and optimistic about dating for the first time in a long time:

From: Melissa
Subject: Thank you

Amy,
I know I normally only write with complaints and fears, but today I just wanted to let you know that things are going great. And it's not because I see us getting married, or I am fantasizing about what might be, it's because I am enjoying what's happening right now. Normally, I get so caught up in being worried about a relationship, I forget to be in it. But this time, I figure whatever is going to happen, is going to happen, so I might as well have fun either way. I don't need to figure out what he is thinking and *I don't need to ask him about it. I guess I just have a lot more faith—and a lot*

more control. We'll see what happens with George but as for today, it's going great!

Thank you, thank you.
Mel

Melissa is right. Whether you believe in God or not, now is the time for faith. You are not a mind reader and you don't need to worry about what is happening between his ears. Melissa had no clue what George was thinking and yet she was staying calm and confident. George was showing all the signs that this was headed toward an exclusive relationship, but Melissa stopped herself from getting too crazy over it. She didn't ask questions. She didn't try to have "a talk." She just sat back and enjoyed what was happening.

I beg you to follow her lead.

Know that this is going in the right direction, and that if you stay busy and distracted, then it's going to happen before you know it.

Relax and get ready for what is probably going to be a real relationship. I can't promise that it will come in Week Six or even Week Seven, or who knows, it could come right now. But what I do know is that you need to believe "que sera, sera." Whatever will be, will be. So have a little faith, relax a little, and know that everything is going to be just fine.

Not Like *That*: Not Yet

Unlike Melissa, I have another client Jen, who after a few weeks of dating her man, decided it was time to Talk. Capital T. Jen is a graphic designer and part-time knitter who makes the prettiest winter hats I have ever seen. She had been dating Nathan, a corporate real estate contractor and weekend surfer, for over a month when she began to get antsy. She called me one afternoon, expressing her concerns, and telling me about her brilliant plan to confront Nathan, explaining how she planned on asking him about it that night at dinner. She had clearly been rehearsing her big speech and how she didn't think it was fair to keep getting closer without some definitions on their relationship. She was going to tell him that she deserved more, and that he needed to "man up." She even added, as a real zinger, that she was dying to have sex with him but just didn't feel like she could do that until they were exclusive.

Talk about showing your cards. And here is probably one of the biggest absolutes of dating: Don't ask him to be exclusive. At this stage in the game, the commitment needs to come from him first. Because the female brain is a funny thing. Any little crack in the foundation of a relationship and it won't take us long to find a way to make it bigger.

If we ask him for an exclusive relationship, we are basically planting a major seed of doubt that we will then water with fear and fertilize with frustration. Then, when any little thing goes wrong, we will say, both to him and most likely to ourselves, "You didn't even want to be with me in the first place!"

Don't do that to yourself. Don't give away that very special power you hold. Remember, he might be the one asking the question, but you are the one who gets to answer. That day, Jen and I talked about her big speech, and I asked her, "Would you rather he ask you first?"

She replied, "Well, of course I would."

I laughed. "Then why are you stopping yourself from getting what you want?"

Far too often, we get in our own way. If things are going well enough in your relationship, and you are convinced that this is someone you want to be with, then do yourself a favor, and wait. You are worth it, and if he is worthy of a relationship, then so is he.

WEEK FIVE: CHOOSE YOUR OWN RELATIONSHIP

This week is all about keeping that one foot in (acting positive, having hope, getting to know him better), and one foot out (holding the reins, seeing other people, playing it cool), so that you don't find yourself rushing into, or rushing him into, a relationship. Remember you are building a very important foundation here; you have spent weeks developing a friendship, and creating real and true intimacy. By holding off on sex, you have instead gotten to know each other emotionally. And in turn, you have proven yourself to be the kind of woman who knows that she deserves a relationship before she offers her greatest gift: her sexuality. Stay true to the work you have done, and stay calm in these last days. The relationship is most likely right around the corner. All you have to do is be patient, be positive, and have faith in what is about to be the greatest adventure of all: the chance to fall in love.

Eight Steps to Everlasting

1. Stay calm and don't make any major moves.
2. Evaluate the relationship and see if this is someone you want to be with.
3. Keep dating other people up until the exclusivity conversation takes place.
4. Keep one foot out (to make sure this is the right person), and one foot in (by letting down your guard more as you get to know each other).
5. Do not initiate the exclusivity talk.

6. These are your final weeks so don't blow it by having sex . . . yet.
7. Don't freak out or start getting nervous or negative if he hasn't brought up being boyfriend and girlfriend.
8. Remember the power that you hold—the power to say yes or no.

Week Six

Exclusivity

Are We a Couple?

I came into the office on a Wednesday morning to find an excited voice mail from my client Tarina. Tarina is the nutritionist who learned that you need to keep dating in order to keep yourself distracted. At that time, she was fully convinced that my client Michael was the one, but after a few short weeks, Michael stopped calling and she had to move on. And she did. About two weeks later, I set her up with Tom, an advertising executive. Six weeks later, I received this message: "Well, Amy, after years of never making it past Week Three, I am finally officially dating someone. Last night, Tom and I went out to dinner and he told me that he had stopped seeing anyone else, and that he hoped I was ready to do the same. I said yes."

Repeat after me—ex-clu-siv-i-ty. This is Week Six.

exclusivity *n.*: belonging to a particular individual and no other; not shared; the first major step to everlasting.

This is the week you've been waiting and working for. This is when he shares that he wants to date you and only you, when he shows that he's willing to be vulnerable for the sake of the relationship. This is a big week for both of you. And it can be really confusing. I can't tell you how many male clients I have who will call me in Week Six, and say, "Amy, help! I like her but I'm not sure what to do next?" You see, you're not the only one who's confused. If your guy starts behaving a little weird here, or you feel like he's hiding something or acting nervous, just know he's about to put himself out on the line . . . big time. The best thing you can do is relax, breathe deep, and know how you're going to respond.

Date Like *This*: Time to Clarify

So, you're sitting across the table from each other. You're lying in his arms. You're walking side by side. You're in the middle of an arcade. And he looks at you, and says, "You know, I really think it's time we get more serious."

You may want to respond with "Yes, yes, yes!" But wait, wait, wait. This is one of the few opportunities you're going to have for a while to define what "more serious" means. Few guys are going to come right out and say, "Dear sweet woman,

I would like to commit to an exclusive relationship with you where we call each other boyfriend and girlfriend and we no longer date other people."

Yeah, probably not. In fact, there a lot of definitions for "more serious," and not all of them are good. Getting more serious could mean "I want to have sex with you," "I will stop having sex with other people, but I am still going to date others," or "I might treat you like a girlfriend but I won't actually call you that."

You don't need to pull out your boilerplate contract at this point and make him agree to every term, but you can take a little pause, and say, "What do you mean by that?"

When you ask him what he means, he might stammer, but if you just give him some space and not offer any suggestions (remember back to Week One—silence is very powerful), he'll be forced to clarify what he's asking you to do. And chances are the easiest words for him to say will be "I'd like for you to be my girlfriend."

Terms are good. It's like George Clooney said in the movie *Up in the Air,* "I stereotype. It's faster." Well, likewise, titles are faster. "Being serious"—who can tell you what that means? Being someone's girlfriend—well, we've been practicing that since boys went from being gross to being cute. So don't lose the opportunity to identify what he means and what he's asking. By simply requesting that he explain, you'll both feel more calm and confident in what you are agreeing to.

Not Like *That*: Dropping Hints

Threats, hints, and ultimatums: They're all the same. Force the issue, and that will get you nowhere. So let's say you're in Week Six, and he hasn't said anything yet. What do you do? You remain calm. Very calm. The kind of calm where you breathe deep and don't say much.

Recently, I had this issue with two of my clients. Remember Paul and Serena? Serena was the ballet dancer and Paul was the only child who could relate to her lonely childhood. Well, after dating for almost two months, Serena began to wonder if Paul was ever going to ask her to make it more serious. I told her to stay calm; I explained that they were only in Week Six, and that this was just the beginning of when you should expect the talk. But Serena was driving herself batty. I understood. Over the last few weeks, they had gotten even closer, and though they had stayed away from sex itself, their emotional intimacy and physical chemistry were definitely on high boil.

I explained to Serena that if she couldn't keep quiet about it, that she should tell Paul that she was really busy at work and to give herself a day or two to calm down. But she didn't. They went out on a Wednesday night and the next day, I received this e-mail from Paul:

From: Paul
Subject: Serena

So Serena and I went out last night, but as we were sitting at dinner, I could tell something was wrong. I asked her if there was something at work, and she said no. I asked if it was her family, and she just shook her head. I thought I had really screwed up or something, so then I asked if it was me and she told me that she was upset that I hadn't asked her if she was dating anyone else. She continued—to be honest, I don't even remember everything she said. But she got pretty excited and basically told me that she didn't know if she could be with me if I wasn't interested in committing. At first I thought she was breaking up with me but then she said how much she liked me and wanted this to become something real. I don't know, Amy, the way she brought it up felt like an ultimatum. Should I be freaked out? I really like her and I totally feel like it's going in the right direction but she felt a little intense last night, like I better ask her out or else. I'm still trying to figure out what just happened to our great night out.

Never a good thing. This is why you don't initiate and you don't push the subject. You stay calm and let him bring it up. Paul was clearly headed in the same direction as Serena, but by jumping in his way, she got in her own way, too.

After the e-mail from Paul, I called Serena and we discussed where her fears were coming from, and how she could salvage the relationship. The next day, she was able to talk to Paul about it, nerves and all. After the conversation, he understood why she had gotten so "excited," and when a week later he brought up the exclusivity talk, they were both more than happy to jump aboard.

You should first know what you're agreeing to, and then be able to calmly, and honestly, reply.

Never Forget That You Have a Choice

Getting a boyfriend is not just about getting *any* boyfriend. It is about meeting someone you trust and respect, someone you are attracted to and can envision a future with. It's not about saying *yes* to the next guy who asks. When we're in the heat of the moment, we can sometimes forget that we are actually being asked a question, which means we have the choice of reply. And we can say either yes or no.

Date Like *This*: Yes or No—It's Up to You

A few summers ago, I was dating this really cute guy I met in Boston. Theo was funny and he sure knew how to romance me. But then one night we were out at dinner, and we started talking about our families, or rather, my family.

I was starting to let him in more, telling him about my relationship with my mom and describing my sister. Theo stared at me blankly, before shrugging his shoulders, and said, "I don't really talk to mine."

I am a firm believer in honesty but Theo's honesty was telling me something. Suddenly it was like all the puzzle pieces fell into place. At first, I just thought Theo was mysterious, but then as I got to know him, I felt like he was hiding something. We all come from varied backgrounds, but I was beginning to think Theo had no intention of telling me about his.

If you're not ready or you realize that this isn't someone you want to be in a relationship with, then you get to stop it here.

I decided to change tactics, and I asked him about his friends. Again, he shrugged, replying, "I really am more into my work than a social life."

I could have ignored it. I could have pretended it didn't apply to our relationship. But here is what I saw: a man who didn't have any interest in family, didn't like to go out with friends, and who would always prefer to be at the office than to be hanging out with me. I remembered all the times Theo had already blown me off for a work dinner or a business trip, and I began to doubt his ability to be in a grown-up relationship where two people were actual partners. He had dated a lot of younger models before me and I got the feeling that Theo liked being able to take off whenever he wanted to.

So, when later that night we went for an evening stroll, and he stopped and kissed me, and said, "You know, I'd like this to be more serious between us. I think maybe it's time we stop seeing other people," I knew I had a real decision in front of me.

Though everything in me screamed, begged, "Yes, yes, I want a boyfriend, yes!" I knew that I wasn't interested in having that with Theo. I told him I would have to think about it, and the next day, I broke it off.

Not Like *That*: Anyone Will Do

My friend Jordan, an event planner in Los Angeles, had been dating Frederick, a CFO for a major restaurant, for almost two months. All she did was complain about him. "He's rude to waiters. He's cheap, and all he talks about is work," she told me. Sure, he looked great on paper—he had the right degree, a good job, they even shared hobbies—but who dates paper?

When I asked why she was dating him, she replied, "Well, he's better than nothing."

Nothing? Boy, did Jordan need to revise her approach—and her strategy. By saying her date was better than nothing, Jordan was actually telling herself that she deserved nothing. And *nothing* could be farther from the truth.

Jordan had to adjust her attitude. She had to understand that she deserved to be with a guy who was charming and attentive, a guy she was interested in and happy to be with, a guy who felt the same way about her. And she had to adjust her strategy and go out with more men. She was wasting her time with Frederick, and she was wasting his time, too. Both of them should have been focused on going out and meeting people they liked, and who would like them back, but Jordan kept going out with ole Freddy. Until finally, he decided to ask for more, and told her that he was already calling her his girlfriend and wanted to make sure it was okay with her.

She said yes. I nearly killed her.

If you don't want to be in the relationship by Week Six, you're probably never going to want to be in the relationship.

Keep It in Perspective

First of all, commitment at this stage only means that he's asking if you would like to stop seeing other people, so put down the bridal magazine. Don't expect rose petals and champagne, though those things would be lovely. Most likely this conversation will happen far more naturally. Rather than both of you acting like nervous teenagers, the conversation should be organic, easy, and always initiated by him.

Depending on the guy, it could range from a simple "I like you. Are you feeling the same about me?" to a much lengthier talk. If you feel like he's assuming that you're together, then don't let him. You shouldn't initiate this conversation but you can always clarify. If he refers to you as his girlfriend, you have every right to ask, "I am?" If it hasn't happened yet, don't freak out, give him some space and time to come to the question on his own. And most important, keep dating. If you are still busy doing things at night and not telling him, he will get the hint. Trust me, guys can be really obtuse unless there is competition.

He's not proposing so you don't need to get teary-eyed and you don't need to go to the restroom to call your mother.

I will never forget when one of my last boyfriends, Adrian, popped the question. We were in Los Angeles, and we had just gone for a hike in Runyon Canyon. We saw another couple walk by us holding hands, and Adrian stopped, turned to me, and said, "I've been thinking about . . . you know, us."

He waited until I responded, "Yes?"

"And I've been thinking maybe it's time, well, it's time to, you know, make it more formal."

I couldn't help but laugh. "Formal?" I looked down at my sweaty workout clothes. "Like I shouldn't be wearing this?"

"No." He chuckled. "I mean official."

Once the talk begins, you are officially in control. Remember, he is not asking for your hand in marriage. Your job is to keep calm and to keep it in perspective.

Commitment is an exciting new adventure, but there's no reason to get ahead of yourself and think this is the be-all and end-all. This is just the first step in what could be a very long journey. Sadly, I know many women who walk away from this conversation confused as to what just happened or embarrassed by their own reply. Yes, it's exciting stuff, and for many of us, we have been waiting for a long time to finally have the shot at being someone's girlfriend again. But that doesn't mean we need to act like we just got crowned Miss America. Instead, act like a composed grown-up being confronted with a real question.

Date Like *This*: What Next?

So, what next? Well, first of all, this is not your signal to go home and have sex with him. This is your signal to end the date with a sweet and tender kiss. Even if you have previously spent the night, do not do so now. You need to get your bearings, and scream to your girlfriends instead of to him. Yes, down the road, you can tell him about how you were on the phone until three A.M. giggling with your girls, but right now you need to maintain your cool . . . and keep your distance. Don't change your behavior overnight.

He just asked you to be his girlfriend; he did not suggest you pack up your things and start storing tampons at his place.

A lot of times, the things that trip us up are our unrealistic and often unacknowledged expectations. But we can avoid that land mine simply by recognizing what we think we are going to get out of the relationship. When my clients Serena and Paul started dating, we had to discuss what that meant for both of them. Unfortunately, you're not going to have me there to moderate, so you need to look at your expectations on your own. Not surprisingly, Serena and Paul had very different ideas about what it meant to be serious. Paul wrote me, "I don't know. I guess I figure it will be like it was before, but now I'll introduce her as my girlfriend."

---

expectations *n.*: 1. to look forward to; regard as likely to happen; anticipate the occurrence or the coming of 2. to suppose or surmise 3. the downfall of many relationships.

Serena's list was a bit longer:

From: Serena
Subject: Expectations

Hey Amy,
So I did what you said and wrote down my list of expectations. What do you think?

1. *We will go on vacations together.*
2. *We will start spending more weekends together.*
3. *He will introduce me as his girlfriend.*
4. *We will change our FB status.*
5. *He will send me flowers this week.*
6. *He will meet my family.*

7. *He wants to get married.*
8. *He wants to have children.*

XO,
S

All I could say in reply was "Whoa, there, girl. Hold your horses!" For us women, once we think things are moving forward, we get ready to run, while our guys are more interested in casual strolls. As soon as I asked Serena to look back at her list and think about what was reasonable and what wasn't, her list went from eight items to two. So, go ahead and write your own, and make an honest evaluation as to what expectations are reasonable, and which need to be thrown out . . . now!

And PS—if you have more than eight, you have *way* too many!

Not Like *This*: Warp Speed Ahead

I'll tell you, there is nothing more terrifying than an obsessive woman, high on the fact that she is now in a relationship. I am sure you have met her. Her language is sprinkled with the word "boyfriend" and no matter what she is talking about—her job, her weekend, the weather—he is somehow a part of it. It is as though her whole identity has been lost in the space of one night. The truth is if you have been doing this work, you have created the kind of habits that will *not* let you become that woman. You have an active social life, without *him,* you have hobbies and work and interests, without *him,* and you also still want some time alone, without *him.* So just because he is your boyfriend, should any of this change? Absolutely not.

But can it? Absolutely. Sadly, I know from my own experience. I have always been outgoing and always thought that my social life and identity were bigger than my involvement with one man, but when Adrian and I first started dating, I nearly forgot that. I figured that since I now had a partner-in-crime, I didn't have time for anyone else. I immediately cancelled the plans I had made with friends to go away for that upcoming weekend. As I told them, "Since Adrian and I just had the big talk this week, I want to be able to see him this weekend to celebrate."

Again, I don't know what I thought had just happened—we were only dating, not getting married. But immediately, I was ready to renege on my friends to have the chance to be with him. Thank goodness I have great friends, who quickly reminded me that if I wanted to celebrate, I should be celebrating with my girls. That's when it hit me: If I was going to give up on my friends in the first week, where would that leave me down the road? Not in a good place, that much I can tell you.

Just because you're dating exclusively does not mean that anything else in your life should change.

There's nothing worse than a woman who turns her back on the rest of her life, and says, oh well, I have a boyfriend, that's all that matters. Don't be that girl. Not only is she a pain to be around, she usually doesn't have that guy for very long, either.

Date Like *This*: Keep It Under Wraps . . . For Now

Just because you had the big conversation doesn't mean that everyone in your world needs to know.

Sure, you'll want to tell your close friends, perhaps a selected coworker, but when you are in the first tenuous days of a new relationship, it is best to go about it quietly and without a lot of phone calls. Why, you wonder? He asked me to be his girlfriend, is that now a secret? No, it's not and it shouldn't be, but your enthusiasm could easily be construed as "acting crazy." Ugh. The word "crazy" is a terrible term that men like to throw at us when we get scared, and act, well . . . crazy. Because the truth is there is nothing more embarrassing than having some guy you just started dating, ask you, "Who have you told about us?" You want a story? Here you go.

About three years ago, my client Jackie was living in L.A. She worked in the film industry, which is where she met Tyler. Tyler was a television executive at a network, and they hit it off immediately. After a month or so, Tyler asked Jackie to be his girlfriend. Good? Good. Jackie was calm and cool and said she would love to be. Good? Good. And then the next day, she went to work and told a small handful of her coworkers in the lunchroom. Well, one of those coworkers happened to live with Tyler's boss's assistant, who then went and told her boss. A few days later, Tyler came in late, and his boss joked, "Hey Tyler, sleeping in with your new girlfriend?"

Tyler was horrified, and even though it wasn't Jackie's fault, it created a bit of a problem for them both. Even if you think it's safe to tell a few people, make sure you know the people well enough to ensure that you won't become their evening gossip.

Not Like *That*: In a Relationship

Oh, Facebook, you confusing feed of useless news and YouTube videos! Ever since Mark Zuckerberg developed the "In a Relationship" update, couples all over the world have been thrown into question. I know marriages that have been rocked by them ("We have been married for five years, why does it say you're 'single'?"). And yes, after five years, you better be asking questions.

In your first weeks of taking it serious, stay away from Facebook!

I know it's tempting. If you're anything like me then you've watched with envy as friends' relationship statuses have changed over time while yours has remained paralyzed, sitting there like a lonely spinster. And then it does change, and of course, you want the world to know. You want to be the girl whose name comes up with a heart following it, and the three little words you have been pining for: In a Relationship.

But not yet.

Though at this point you may be Facebook friends with your new boyfriend, this is also an area in which he should be the one to initiate. Let him be the one to ask or to change it on his own. Although I would be wary of any man who raced home that same night and immediately connected you two through a relationship. Allow the relationship to get its footing, make sure this is something that feels right and comfortable to you both, and then after a few weeks, if things are going good, see if he brings it up. And what does it mean to him when you don't bring it up? That you could care less. That you are too busy and have too much going on in your life to obsess over something so silly as Facebook. Instead of coming off as the desperate girl with her finger hovering over the keyboard, you become the woman who is confident enough to know that FB statuses mean little, unless you've got the real thing.

And if by month three, he still hasn't said anything, then I would go ahead and mention it. You can make it a casual statement, like "So, I've been thinking about changing my Facebook status." But at this stage in the game, no changes are good changes. So don't get in there and feel like you have to mix things up. In the end, the more you try to initiate (and not influence) how quickly or slowly the relationship is moving, the more likely you are to create drama. As my client Jessica had to learn.

Jessica and Michael, one of my clients who had previously dated the overbearing Melanie, had begun to see each other more seriously. Jessica was ten years younger than Michael and certainly much more active on Facebook than he was, but they were both still on it, and had become FB friends after they had been dating a month. The weekend after they decided to stop dating other people, Jessica went on and put herself "In a Relationship," and then added Michael to the link.

When he wrote me about it, I almost died.

From: Michael
Subject: Facebook

Hi Amy,
How are you? So I have a quick question for you. Sadly, I'm not a regular Facebook user (really dating myself here, huh?), so I was a little confused when I got a message from Jessica saying that she was in a relationship with me. Is this normal? I mean, I feel like we just started this thing and I don't know that everyone in my business and personal contacts needs to know that. But I also don't want to be rude. If people normally put it on right away, I will. I really like Jessica and I don't want her to be offended.

Regards,
M.

Luckily for Jessica, Michael was naïve enough to not know just how forward Jessica was being. I told him to tell Jessica that he wasn't comfortable making that change so public yet, but to give it another month, and he would love to tell everyone about it. Since I had already reached out to Jessica, she understood, and once she realized what she was doing, that Michael was someone who used Facebook for work as much as his personal life, she felt terrible that she had put him in such an awkward position.

Very few things in the world are as personal and as public as Facebook. Always make sure that you have set your privacy settings to protect yourself and anyone you bring into your life from embarrassing photos, silly posts, or anything that you wouldn't want your new boyfriend's boss to find. Even if you're already friends with your guy on Facebook, you need to remember just how many people can and will have access to your information, and you need to tread lightly . . . both in and out of a relationship.

Date Like *This*: You Can Start Slackening the Reins

So here's the deal. You have basically just been through dating boot camp—you have learned to hold the reins, keep your distance, let him initiate, and always make sure you have kicked the ball to his court.

Dating should begin to feel like second nature, and you should be applying these principles with ease.

You are now no longer in those early stages of romance. You are in the far more relaxed and mutual environment of a relationship. Does that mean you always need to wait for his call? No. And does that mean you can now start asking him out from time to time? Yes.

Because the operative part of the words "girlfriend" and "boyfriend" is "friend." You are not just dating each other, you are also becoming good friends. And so just as you would with anyone else in that category, you can start letting your hair down a little. You can start doing more casual things—like watching a ballgame at home on a Sunday afternoon—and you can start taking a little bit more initiative. Again, a little bit (not a lot) more. What does that mean? If, say, you read a great review of a movie you want to see, then feel free to forward it to him and find out if he's interested. This doesn't mean you go overboard. Take the time and consider the situation to see if it's right.

I know when I first started dating my ex it was fun to relax a bit, but I also knew that I needed to *keep myself in check*. I needed to make sure I wasn't asking him out every day or texting him all the time (one of my bigger issues in dating). But I could and would call him up after work to see if he wanted to catch dinner, or if there was a show I wanted to see, I would ask if he wanted to join. Now, please keep in

TAKE THE TEMPERATURE

Does initiating feel comfortable and right for where you're at, or does it make either of you feel awkward—and by either of you, I mean you, too? Before you let go of the reins completely or hold on so tight that dating doesn't feel natural, see what works at this point in your relationship.

1. Do you feel comfortable calling him up?
2. Have you asked him out to dinner and, if so, how did he respond?
3. Has he noticed that you have begun to initiate more?
4. Does he respond to your suggestions?
5. Does he ignore you when you mention a restaurant or some place you would like to go?
6. Can he also relinquish a little control, or does he like to be the only planner on deck?
7. Do you feel comfortable enough around him to express your opinion and what you would like to do?
8. Are you keeping yourself in check—not calling or texting him more than once every two days? And not asking him out more than once a week?

mind that some people move slower and therefore, they might be a little more cautious. The change in pace might throw him for a moment. Remember you have not asked him out once up until this point! But if he can't handle you asking him to dinner, then chances are he isn't really mature enough to handle a real relationship.

Being exclusive isn't about being boyfriend and girlfriend in name alone. It's about building a partnership between two people, starting with the growing friendship at its core. Something you should both be very much a part of creating.

Not Like *That*: Don't Let the Horses Run

Just because you're loosening the reins a bit doesn't mean you get to let the relationship fly. Far too often, women mistake being in a relationship with being in control, and not in the right way. As soon as they hear "boyfriend," they think their job is to schedule weekends, figure out what you're both going to wear, and in general direct the relationship like, well . . . a general. Talk about losing a guy in ten days!

Though at this point, your new guy is becoming more than just a friend, you need to remember that he's still a man. It might be time to relax and let your hair down a bit, but it is not time to do a 180-degree turn, going from playing it cool to playing it psycho. Yes, you might be initiating a little bit more, and by that, I mean once a week, tops. But that doesn't mean you should be calling him every day, or setting up dates for weeks or months in advance. You need to remain calmer than ever before. Which means you shouldn't be discussing holidays, family functions, or anything that smacks of "I want to get married, and have decided in less than two months that I want to get married to you."

No bueno. And if you want to see how that makes the guy feel, just read the following e-mail I received from one of my clients Julian. Julian had been seeing Marta, our Italian food publicist from Week Two, for over a month. Julian was a CNN journalist who traveled quite a bit for his job, but was hoping to start slowing that down in order to settle down. He was smitten with Marta from the start and it was no surprise when Marta wrote me saying that they had decided to start dating exclusively. But then three days later, I received the following from Julian:

From: Julian
Subject: Women

Amy,
I don't know what to say. I feel like up until last week I was dating the most amazing woman—confident, successful, gorgeous, and fun—and then the minute it started to get serious, she changed. She keeps calling and texting me, and last weekend, she got upset when I couldn't meet up with her and her friends for brunch. I wasn't even sure if there was going to be another guy there, which made me even more concerned. It's like she thinks we're married. I've really enjoyed her company but

I'm afraid she's looking for a much faster commitment than I'm prepared to give. I was going to break up with her tonight but thought I should check in with you first.

Regards,
Julian

Wow. Marta was way off her mark, and, I was concerned, off her rocker, too. When I questioned her about her behavior, Marta explained that she had been trying so hard not to be the aggressor (her usual role in relationships), she just got ahead of herself once she felt like she could initiate a bit more. And therein lies the big difference: You can begin to initiate a bit more, *not* a *lot* more.

By now, you should know your own boundaries, and you should also be getting to know his. Pay attention to what he is comfortable with, and what he is not.

Keep in mind that these are just the first few days of what will hopefully be a long relationship. Enjoy them, savor them. Just as there was no need to rush to this point, there is no need to rush past it, either.

WEEK SIX: CHOOSE YOUR OWN RELATIONSHIP

Dating is about learning to overcome our vulnerabilities and insecurities. That's true for all of us. Through my own scrapes and bruises (and downright open flesh wounds), I came to a point where I finally listened to the same rules I have taught my clients. When I realized I'm worth a guy who is wonderful and respectful and wants to be with me, I was ready to move forward to Week Six with confidence and calm. And you will be, too.

But first you need to make sure it is with the right person. This is your last chance off the *Titanic*; now is a great time to pause and see whether this is what you really want. If he's treating you right, and if you know he's someone you want to be with, then relax and know he will ask you when the time is right—if not in Week Six, then soon. But if he does pop the question (not the big one, this is only a little one, remember), then take that pause and be sure to clarify what he is asking for. Once you are in that much-anticipated relationship, remember that you can relax a bit and take more initiative. That doesn't mean asking him out all the time, announcing it to the world, posting it on Facebook, or becoming someone that you're not. If you have done the work, and completed our dating boot camp up to this point, you should be ready to embark on a fun, healthy, mutually ex-clu-sive romance based on a growing friendship . . . which might one day turn into more.

Eight Steps to Everlasting

1. Never, ever, ever initiate the exclusivity conversation.
2. Stay calm and stay alert.
3. When he asks about getting more serious, clarify what he means and what he is looking for.
4. Remember, he is only asking you to be his girlfriend, not his wife. Keep it in perspective.
5. Still no sex—let your relationship find its footing first.
6. Do not change your life . . . or your Facebook status.
7. You can start initiating more—asking him out, calling him—but keep yourself in check. No more than one call per day and one invite per week.
8. Enjoy this time and stay present. No need to rush anything!

Week Seven

S-E-X

Now Can I Let Loose?

(Yes, I know you're reading this chapter first!)

Good things come to those who wait. And you've done such a good job waiting that you and your partner are about to be rewarded. Big time. If you're in an exclusive relationship and dating someone you trust, someone you feel intimate enough with to take it to the next level, then get ready for some delicious fun. Because sex with someone you are falling for, and who is falling for you, can be absolutely wonderful. Enjoy it! Indulge! You two have done an amazing job building a strong foundation and romancing each other into exclusivity. Now you get to celebrate those efforts by having some fun in the bedroom.

Sex can be wild and wonderful, but don't fall into that "I can't live without him" trap.

Many of us feel (even if we don't admit it) that sex is the way to a man's heart. We ignore the science, which proves that the minute we have sex with someone, we produce a chemical (thank you, oxytocin!) that emotionally bonds us to our lover. We pretend that sex can be casual and then we get hurt when it is.

But what happens once you're in a relationship? How do you have sex and still maintain some distance? How do you create boundaries to fight back against those nasty chemicals that can quickly take you from being "Ms. Cool" to "Ms. I Can't Live Without Him"? The secret is protecting yourself from your own worst enemy: those tricky little hormones.

You do not have to be at the mercy of your hormones. You can counterbalance them. Because you have something stronger than the chemicals pulsing through you: You have your brilliant and powerful mind, which can create a plan of action, identifying what you're comfortable with, and what's going to make you nervous. So you need to make sure you use that brain to navigate the wild world of whoopee. Did I just use the word "whoopee?" Yes, I did. Because as I said before, the male mind hasn't changed since the 1950s, and while that doesn't mean we have to go back to wearing pearls and baking pot pies, we do need to respect that, in many ways, the rules haven't changed, either.

Here's the secret your grandmother never told you: People did have sex back then—they just approached it differently. And they were *way* more successful at it (more marriages, less divorce). So let's find out how you can let loose in the bedroom and still hold on to your power.

Sex Like *This*: With the Right One

Some of us have had our fair share of casual sex and that's all well and good, but if you want this relationship to be real and lasting, the sex can't be casual. Because once given, sex can never be taken back.

That's why it is so important to be sure that you are doing it with someone with whom you feel confident, safe, and open enough to have the conversations that sex demands. That is the kind of guy that you should want to be in a relationship with. If you get jittery around deciding where to go for dinner, imagine how you'll feel having to use the word "rubber."

If you don't feel comfortable having the protection conversation with this man, then you shouldn't be having sex with him. Period.

For many of you, none of this is new or awkward. You might be totally comfortable being open with a one-night stand, but things can get more complicated with someone that you really like. And then there is that dangerous thought process: "Well, if we're exclusive . . ."

I'm going to give it to you straight. You just started, so until six months go by and everybody goes in for his or her sexy romantic blood work, keep a Jimmy on it. And yes, you should feel comfortable enough to say that to him. Before you do something you regret, or with someone who didn't deserve you in the first place, make sure that you feel 100 percent comfortable and that he is 100 percent safe.

Before you even go there, you need to spend some time deciding if you are secure enough with him to take it to that next level. How would you respond to the following eight questions?

1. Do you feel safe and relaxed with him?
2. Do you trust what he says?
3. Do his actions back up his words?
4. Could you comfortably talk to him about sex and protection?
5. Has he respected your wishes up until this point?
6. Does he seem to respect sex, i.e. not treat it lightly?
7. Does he make you feel good about yourself—physically and emotionally?
8. Do you share similar values and ideas about sex?

If you answered no to *any* of these questions, you're not ready for sex with this guy . . . or he might not be the right one after all.

Not Like *That*: Bad Timing

You don't have to have sex just because it's Week Seven. It needs to be the right time. Are you on your period? Wrong time. Have you just had a lovely and romantic evening together? Right time. Do you have to work in the morning? Wrong time.

Don't think that this is the right time just because you've had the exclusivity conversation. Men and women approach sex and relationships differently. You may be ready. But is he?

Remember Francesca and Peter, the couple embarking on a great friendship after just a few dates? Well, after some time, a great romance bloomed. Then they decided to get serious. Too serious. And they both kind of freaked out. Francesca wrote me a week after they decided to make it official.

From: Francesca
Subject: Pete

Oh, Amy. What to do? So last week, Pete and I had the big talk and we agreed that we wanted to start dating only each other. It was so romantic. We were walking along the Potomac River and the sun was setting and I couldn't have imagined it better. But then after that, I kept waiting for him to call and it felt like he was backing off. I invited him over for dinner on Friday but then he said he had to work. He called me the next day and apologized and said he wanted to make it up to me. I am going over for dinner tonight and I am tempted to sleep with him (I've been tempted this whole time!) but I'm not sure what that would mean if he's not feeling it anymore.

Pete was still feeling it; he had just gotten a little case of cold feet. That's all perfectly natural. He had been single a long time so he wasn't exactly sure how to feel or what to do—it had been years since he had called *anyone* his girlfriend. See, you're not the only one who gets nervous! A lot of men get into relationships not knowing how they're supposed to behave, or it's been so long, they've nearly forgotten. Though they might act strange at first, understand that they are just finding their balance. But know this: *Having sex will not help.* It will only confuse the situation. And you can't have two people freaking out. Stay calm and wait for him to join you. Wait until the moment is relaxed, and you feel confident in what you are about to do. Once you have both found your bearings in this new and exciting relationship, you can consider having the S-E-X.

If the guy is acting a little funny, you need to act calm. It's like approaching a barking dog; if both of you are scared, one of you is going to get hurt.

Sex Like *This*: Have Some Fun

This should go without saying, but sometimes we need a reminder that this is a time for fun.

If you've had the honest sex conversation (see below), if you feel comfortable having sex with him, if you have set your boundaries in and out of the bedroom, then I say, go for it, sister. It might not be quite the time to bring out the whips and chains (and for those of you who are into this sort of thing, save it for later), but you should be enjoying each other, staying up late, getting it on, and sleeping in the next morning, appreciating the après dessert called cuddling.

Week Seven is not only about getting to know each other sexually, it's also about building physical and emotional intimacy. It's about lying in bed, talking about your families and your dreams, finding that perfect part of his neck where your head fits just right. It's about learning how to caress each other without tickling and showing him the birthmark on your belly. As intimacy develops, you should feel more and more comfortable—whether your clothes are on or not. He should be making you feel like you are one of the most beautiful women in the world. And you should be to him—you're in his bed.

Far too many women get so caught up in the "Should we or shouldn't we?" or "We did but should we have?" that we forget that sex by nature is supposed to be fun.

The first few weeks after Adrian, my Los Angeles boyfriend, and I started dating exclusively were some of the best days of our relationship. His apartment became my four-star hotel where we ordered in, watched movies in bed, and made love. Those early days of sex and romance are some of the best ones, so relax, enjoy them, cherish them—you are creating memories together. Ones, which if all goes well, will help to build a very important future.

Not Like *That*: Rushing Heart First

Sex is amazing. People write songs about it. Entire cultures are devoted to its celebration. And let's face it, it's much more fun to do than, well . . . pretty much anything else. It can be hot and heavy. It can be sweet and romantic. It can be whatever you and your partner want it to be.

Sex is a uniquely personal and wonderful experience. But the other funny little thing about sex is that it can also jumble up an otherwise very intelligent brain.

Think about it: For the last seven weeks, you have spent time and energy establishing a very important, well-crafted relationship. It's like you've been building one of those little model boats. You've carefully attached and glued the delicate pieces together. You stayed calm even when it looked like it was going to fall apart. You painted the little windows and doors, proud of your hard work and dedication. And then once it was all pieced together, you dropped it in the middle of the Pacific Ocean.

And that is exactly what you will be doing to the relationship if you rush into sex. That doesn't mean you shouldn't have it, but it does mean you should think it through as carefully and honestly as you have thought through the first six weeks of the relationship. And if you do, the reward will be *wonderful*. Not only will you be in an exclusive relationship with the right man for you, you will build a fulfilling physical connection as well.

The Conversation

When you do decide you're ready, first have the conversation. Congratulations! You have finally arrived at a conversation *you* can initiate. Because this conversation shows that you are a responsible woman who wants to make sure she is emotionally and physically safe before she proceeds to the bedroom. This is not something you *can* bring up; this is something you *must* bring up. A true lady doesn't just hop into bed without laying down the game rules. So first establish what yours are: Are you secure in the terms of your new relationship? Do you know what kind of protection you plan to use? What, if any, are your concerns or worries about engaging in sex at this point?

There is a time for words and a time for action. This is the time to use your words before anyone gets any action.

If there is anything in your sexual past (and this includes STDs) that needs explanation then be up front with your partner so that he understands if sex is tricky for you. Your best friend would never judge you for this, and neither should your lover. Speaking up will help you determine whether this is someone who can handle intimacy.

By now, you should have had the exclusivity conversation. Then, and only when you're ready, can you have the second big conversation: the one about sex. But what does that look like? First, you should feel comfortable and confident enough with your guy to bring up the topic. Second, this is a conversation you can initiate, so have at it, girls. Be in charge!

The most important thing is that you both agree on the question of safety. Though you might change your birth control methods later, now is the time to set ground rules: condoms, the Pill, etc. And until everyone is tested, you shouldn't be riding bareback. And that's the truth!

Next, before you start getting jiggy, you need to *re*-confirm that this is a mutually exclusive relationship. And by mutual I mean, *you will only be having sex with each other.* You might feel like you've already had that talk, but chances are the little detail "I will not have sex with anyone else" did not actually come up in that first romantic conversation about how much you like spending time together. No, that time is now.

The sex convo is not a romantic discussion; it is a technical one.

And finally, if you have any fears or concerns about sex, you need to share them. This goes back to the question of emotional intimacy. Before you get physically intimate, the emotional bond needs to be firm. If you've had any bad experiences in the past, or have any physical issues that can make sex a little scary, let him know. Again, if you feel comfortable enough to have sex with this man, then you better feel comfortable enough to explain any anxiety you have around sex. And by doing so, you are showing self-respect, and are saving yourself from worry or paranoia in the future.

Last year, I worked with a client Connie, who had been single for many years until she met someone on her own. Connie was a flight attendant and so she thought a matchmaker would help her to find someone on the ground, but then she met Sebastian on one of her flights and things took off (pun intended). Once they started dating, Connie asked if she could still e-mail me for dating advice, to which I was more than happy to say yes!

Connie and her new boyfriend had just started seeing each other exclusively, but she wanted to hold off on sex until she felt they were in the right place. I agreed with her move until I got the following e-mail:

From: Connie
Re: Ooops

Hey Amy,
Well, I was doing really well there for a while, but I think I might have blown it this weekend. Sebastian and I went back over to his place on Thursday and I ended up staying the night. And having sex. He was just as surprised as I was. We didn't use protection and then it was really awkward in the morning because we both had to get up and go to work. I felt like I was doing the walk of shame and I had to keep reminding myself that he was my boyfriend. I waited, so I'm not really sure what went wrong—I mean obviously we should have used protection, but why didn't we?

XOXOXO,
Connie

Why didn't they? Because they didn't plan ahead. The first time you have sex with someone should never be a surprise. It shouldn't be like, "Oh, one minute we were having Peking duck, and then, oops, we were getting it on!" No. The first time you have sex should be with the same measured pace with which you have gone on dates, and slowly progressed to this point. Don't stop that pace now by rushing forward like two lunatics. Sex should be well-thought-out, discussed, and sensibly considered. And then when you're ready, stepped into with care and caution.

FUN FACT: Sex isn't a sample sale, so don't rush in; it's one of the most important acts two humans can share. If it doesn't feel right, then don't do it. Because though there might be exchanges on this item, there is no full refund.

Sex Like *This*: Setting the New Pace

No, I'm not talking about how many times a week you guys have sex. I mean really, girls, that one's up to you. But there's still a pace to be set and kept, and that is how much time you're spending with each other. I get it: You're feeling it, you're falling into what could be easily defined as "love," but that doesn't mean you should move in after the first two weeks of being exclusive. It's important to keep your old life intact even as this new one emerges.

When Adrian and I started dating exclusively, and exclusively having sex, soon after, I found myself going days and then weeks without seeing my apartment. It started to seem weird that I was shelling out so much money for a place that I only saw once a week. And here is where my brain started to go: I thought, why shouldn't we just move in with each other? He obviously wants me at his place all the time.

I am lucky that I called my best friend, Danielle, before sharing my plan with him. Danielle instantly replied, "What is wrong with you? You think you're going to save money by moving in with someone you just started dating? How about you just stop spending all week at his apartment?"

You need your space, and you need to utilize that space.

And if he always wants you to come to his place, gently remind him that you pay rent at yours, too, so it might be nice for you both to see it sometime. I know a lot of guys who always want it on their turf, but you have a home, too—don't abandon it just because you like the way your toothbrush looks next to his. And if he doesn't want to join you, then fine. He'll get to sleep alone. That's the deal. Don't break it.

Not Like *This*: A Crazy Person

Sometimes we get in our heads, and make decisions based on what we think is happening, rather than on reality. Stop the story, ladies. It is not good for you, and it certainly doesn't look good on you, either.

---

crazy *adj.*: intensely enthusiastic; infatuated; impatient; the best way to scare off a guy.

I had just started representing Dana when on a first date she claimed to have met "her match." I warned her not to get too excited, but despite my protests she and Nigel really seemed to be into each other. Nigel is my commitment-loving client who had been turned off in the past by women who slept with him on the first date. But Dana and Nigel were taking it slow and steady. His interest seemed to be increasing and he shared with me that he didn't want to see anyone else, weeks before he told her. Not long after, they started dating exclusively and then began sleeping together. It was all going well, until Dana started to question everything. She sent me daily e-mails asking what I thought it meant if he didn't call her by a certain hour, and she e-mailed him by eleven A.M. if he hadn't contacted her first. She worried if Nigel didn't ask her out every night. She would get upset if he was late for a date, and then during an otherwise romantic dinner for two, she told him she didn't know where the relationship was going. She said she deserved more, and that Nigel clearly didn't know how or want to commit to a woman. She explained that she was happy to start seeing other people again, and that maybe that's what Nigel secretly wanted, too. She started to cry. Nigel was totally floored. He wrote me later that week to explain.

From: Nigel
Subject: Surprised

Hi Amy,
Well, I was pretty shocked about what happened the other night so I wasn't sure how to reply to your e-mail. Clearly, Dana has been in touch with you. Look, I know dating and romance are hard for all of us, so I certainly didn't want to take Dana to task for her behavior, but I also felt that for someone her age (she's not twenty-one, you know), she should have known better. I am not sure what was going through her head, I'm not sure I want to know, but I

do know that she really spoiled a good thing. I told her that I would meet her for lunch but I'm just not sure I want to be with someone who doesn't know how to handle things. . . . Life can certainly get much bumpier than this. I'd be happy to chat with you after we talk, but as for now, I think I just want to take some time away from it.

Thanks,
N.

That was a bummer. And completely avoidable. It sounded like Dana was enacting a play in her mind that she decided Nigel should attend. This happens too often. If you're freaking out, freak out . . . to your mom, your therapist, your friend, but do not freak out to him. Run it by them to see if your fears are rational, or if you are overwhelming yourself with needless worry. Nigel was right about how immature Dana's behavior was, and she lost a potentially wonderful relationship because of it.

I know sex can seem scary. And falling for someone can be downright terrifying, but this is the time for your most calm and confident face. Far too often, women start to feel vulnerable after sex, and then they fall apart. If you really want to confuse your man, start crying at the dinner table for no apparent reason. That'll make him want to stay.

Sex Like *This*: The Analysis Isn't Over

Just as you set boundaries this week, you also need to take a small step back to evaluate whether this is going in the right direction. Sure, you're having fun in bed, but that doesn't mean that you need to lose your head. (Yes, I know that rhymes.) Now, more than ever, watch for signs as to whether your guy is falling in love or falling in lust. Have things changed for the better since you started to have sex? Or have they changed for the worse? Be honest and list what you've noticed in the relationship since you did the deed.

I know that all along I've been telling you, "Let him initiate," but that doesn't mean he gets to dictate. By now, you should know if you are dating a bully, but sometimes it's amazing how good guys can be at hiding this particular quality. Since many of us look for strong men who take the bull by the horns (particularly, if we're looking for someone who knows how to initiate), we might miss some of his other more, shall we say, dictator-like qualities. Just as you shouldn't boss him around, he shouldn't be bossing you, either.

A relationship is all about partnership: two equals working together to create a united pair. But if one of the equals thinks he or she is in charge, that is not a partnership. Do not be goaded by someone just because you like him.

For as many background checks as I perform on clients, they don't actually show their true colors until I see them in a relationship. I had been working with Ryan for almost a year when he finally started seeing someone he liked. Maria is our HR executive from chapter one who went out with the confident guy until she realized he was cocky and had a taste for hostesses. But Ryan was different. Though a strong, confident type, he also acted laid-back in their relationship. They had a nice pace going with dinners out, weekends together, and enough time apart to take care of their own lives. But once they were officially dating, Ryan asked Maria out all the time. She started to feel like he was needy, and not necessarily in love. Maria backed off, and then Ryan accused Maria of cheating. She wrote me the next day:

From: Maria
Subject: Ryan

I am so sad, Amy. Last night Ryan turned into a crazy man. As I told you last week, I had begun to say no a lot of the times he asked me out—which wasn't to say that I didn't see him a lot. It was just that he asked me out so much! It was getting to feel a little strange. But then when he wanted to go away for the weekend, and I couldn't (I have a work function on Saturday), he lost it on me. He said he knew I was seeing someone else and that I should just come clean with it. I'm so upset. I'm not sure if this relationship is worth repairing or if Ryan might need to work on himself before he starts dating anyone else. Should I try again with him?

Demanding someone's time or obsessing over them doesn't make them feel like you care about them. It just makes them think you're lonely, or worse, crazy.

From the way Ryan was acting, I had to say no. It did not seem like he was emotionally mature enough to be in a relationship with anyone, and Maria certainly didn't need to contend with that baggage. The same goes for you. You might be in a relationship, but you should still be in charge of your schedule and your life. Just because you are dating does not mean that whatever he says goes. It means that you are now one-half of an equal partnership, in which you both have boundaries, your own space, and within reason, the freedom to choose how you spend your time.

Once sex is introduced in the mix, you want to make sure that he isn't being surreptitious and undoing all your hard work. Now is the time to make sure that he is still making the same romantic overtures that he started with—this is no time for slacking, for either of you. You want to make sure that he is still planning great dates, he is asking you out for future events, he is inviting you to spend time with his friends, and maybe, just maybe, he is mentioning his family.

My friend Lisette has been dating a guy for the last month or so, and they basically split their time between his bed, hanging with their friends, and spending romantic nights to-

IS IT LOVE OR LUST?

Once you start doing the nasty, there are going to be some new signs about where this relationship is heading. So take a step back and look at his behaviors:

1. Are you still going out on dates? Is he romancing you more than ever?
2. Does he want to do more than just hang out at his/your place?
3. Does he make sex his top priority or does he seem more interested in getting to know you?
4. Has he respected your requests around sex regarding protection and any other boundaries you have discussed?
5. Does he consider your needs and opinions, or does he try to bully you?
6. Does he go out of his way to see you by making sure he plans in advance?
7. Do you feel beautiful and special in his presence?
8. Is he calling you his girlfriend?

None of these things should change just because you have sex, and if they have, then rein in the sexual behavior and start navigating the relationship back to its earlier course—more compliments, more respect, and more nights out on the town . . . and not just in his bedroom.

gether where she feels like he is still trying to get her to sleep with him—even though she already has. None of these behaviors should stop just because the nooky happened.

Not Like *That*: Woo What?

Far too many women think that once they are officially dating the wooing is over. No way. The games have just begun. Just as you need to be on your guard now more than ever, he needs to be on his best behavior.

Having sex does not mean the end of romance; in fact, it should be just the beginning.

Don't settle for less than what you're worth. If you don't feel like you're getting what you want from the relationship, you have every right to pull back . . . or to leave.

Last year, my client Bree, the landscape architect from Los Angeles, finally met the perfect guy. Everything was going well, but once they started a more serious relationship, she felt like Mr. Perfect was turning into Mr. Rut. Thankfully, Bree knew what to do. She wrote me later.

From: Bree
Subject: Advice for others

So I just told Darren that I was going away for the weekend, and booked myself a spa vacation. One of my girls might join me but either way that got his attention. He invited himself, but I told him that from time to time, I just like to escape the city and have a little "me" time. I told him that when I got back into town, perhaps we could have dinner. After weeks of takeout at his place, he met me at my house, took me to a beautiful restaurant, and then came home to spend the night with me. When he invited me to his place on Friday, I told him that I already had a work engagement but that I would love to do something on Saturday. He got the hint without me even having to say anything. We've still been spending quality time at his place but I think he's realized that I am not the kind of woman who just wants to sit (or lay) around.

Kudos to you, Bree. If you have done the legwork, and learned how to build the structure of your relationship, while still allowing him to fill in all those lovely details, you should be feeling just as confident and self-assured.

WEEK SEVEN: CHOOSE YOUR OWN RELATIONSHIP

So it's happening. You're in a real relationship, and it looks like you might just be falling in love. Well, before we move on to the closer, Week Eight, let's stop and make sure you are where you're supposed to be. Are you feeling more comfortable with him? Are you exploring whatever level of intimacy feels right? If you are spending the night at his place, are you taking it slow—not moving anything into his apartment, still spending at least three to four nights at your own place, and still upholding your commitments to work, friends, and your hobbies? And most important, are you having fun?

A lot of great things come to fruition in Week Seven, and a lot of them are the products of your hard work. You've spent the last seven weeks becoming a stronger woman and partner, and you have finally learned not only how you should be treated, but also how to ask for it without saying anything. And you didn't have to change a single thing about yourself. You just had to learn how to change your behaviors in the first eight weeks to everlasting. Let me tell you a little secret: You had it in you the whole time. By now, you are aware of the incredible power that comes with being a woman.

Eight Steps to Everlasting

1. Once you start having sex, you can't take it back, so make sure that you are ready and want to move forward with your partner.

2. If you decide to have sex, you should first have the conversation. If you don't feel comfortable having "the talk," you're probably not comfortable enough to have sex.
3. Keep yourself safe and protected until you have been together long enough to really trust each other . . . and to have had blood tests.
4. Don't stop working on the emotional connection just because you are now focusing on the physical one.
5. Set boundaries for your time, how often you stay at his place, and how often you go out together—he should still be wooing you.
6. If you have any concerns or questions related to sex or your sexual histories, ask him. Here's the one area where taking the reins means asking questions.
7. Keep your commitments—to friends, to work, to your hobbies, and to yourself.
8. Continue to evaluate the growth and promise of the relationship. You shouldn't be dating anyone just to date him. Not to mention having sex with him!

Week Eight

Enjoy the Relationship—Don't Lose Yourself in It

Now What?

Congratulations! By this point, you should be settling into the first throes of a real relationship. This is the week where you set the rhythm, establishing the pace and habits that make having a boyfriend fun and fulfilling. You're starting to get comfortable with the relationship that is clearly forming between you. You probably even refer to each other as boyfriend and girlfriend, and if you're anything like me, you secretly mouth "I have a boyfriend!" to yourself in the mirror. Yes, you do. But here's where the real work begins.

Think of Week Eight as the first week of the rest of your life, or at least, for as long as this relationship lasts. Because the choices you make today will echo resoundingly throughout your future.

Does that mean you need to play some silly game or act like someone other than who you are? No way. But you do need to realize that while you are someone's girlfriend, that's not all you are. You walked into this relationship with a fully formed personality, and if you have read anything I wrote, a fully formed social life. Now is not the time to forget that, but rather to see how your world fits with your new beau's world.

Because if you forgo the rest of your life, chances are you will wake up six months from now with no friends and a very bored boyfriend who's wondering what happened to the vivacious, independent woman he was dating only months before. There are ways to make love last, and the first of which is to remain the person he fell in love with. He's falling for the person you are today—the woman with friends, and ambitions, and hobbies, and dreams that don't always include him. And he wants to be with that woman. That's why he committed in Week Six, and why he's telling his mom about you. Not because you are some wallflower whose only identity is being his girl. No, he committed because you made an impression on him, so don't stop.

Date Like *This*: Don't Lose the Reins

If you drop the reins now you will never get them back. Love is a funny thing. It takes us for a ride, and if we do it right, we never have to get off. We can take that pony right into the sunset.

Getting into a relationship may be tricky; staying in one is even tougher.

If you've done the work and know what you're looking for in a man, and then you find that special guy, the only thing that stands between you and love are the choices that you make. I'm not saying that he can't and won't screw it up. Plenty of guys make their own mistakes on the way to love. But here's the secret: If you make the right choices, you have a better chance to make it last. Which is why I'm being so annoying about the reins. This is not the time to hand over all control and watch the relationship run wild. No, this is the time to pay attention, and counteract anything that doesn't feel right. Like Bree did in Week Seven, if there is some new habit or routine that you feel isn't right for you or the relationship, you need to reject it.

Women usually think that talking through an issue will resolve it, but often we end up saying *no* and doing *yes*. Remember, actions are more important than words, especially at this stage of the relationship. Instead of making him sit down and have a long, arduous conversation about something that's bothering you, change your behaviors so that he is forced to change his. That doesn't mean you can't voice your real and genuine concerns. If you fear he is cheating on you or if he is doing something that hurts you or makes you feel bad, you need to tell him how you feel. But you don't need to tell him how you feel *all the time*. More often than not, all it will take is a behavior change on your part to create a behavior change on his. Take a look at each situation, run it by a trusted friend, and see what will speak louder: actions or words.

And keep in mind that this applies to both the big things and the little things. Recently, my client Jill told me she felt weird that her new guy kept trying to come over after drinking with the guys. Though they were progressing in other ways that proved their relationship wasn't just a booty call, his behaviors still made her feel that way. She explained that she put an end to it by not answering the phone after a certain hour. He tried one more time, and then he got the hint, and never called from a bar again.

That's because Jill was holding the reins. She knew her values and boundaries in the relationship, and she didn't need a PowerPoint presentation to get her point across. She just didn't pick up the phone.

Not Like *That*: Act Like You've Won the Lotto

We get excited. It happens. But remember, he's a boyfriend, not the winning Lotto number. Many relationships make it to eight weeks, but not to twelve. And many make it to twelve, but not twenty-four. I know that's the cold hard truth, but if you act like you have won an Oscar because you got a boyfriend, both you and he will ultimately be disappointed.

Just as you have done before, make sure you're getting

what you want from him. Ask yourself where you see this relationship going. How would you like it to grow? And does he have the qualities to support that? As you did in the beginning, list the things you think are most important to you. Don't refer to your first list until you are done with this version. Once it's complete, check the first list to see which qualities you wanted then and which you want now. Have they changed? Have they been influenced by the guy you are dating? That's not a bad thing, but you do need to distinguish where he's making the grade and where he's not. By recognizing the gaps between what you want and what you have, you can also set your expectations. Say you want someone who cares about the world, but you're dating a man who's more focused on what's in front of him. That doesn't mean he's not the perfect guy, but you might need to have more patience or adjust your expectations around the subject. Okay, on to the new list. What does yours look like?

I revised my list when I was dating Adrian and I was surprised by how the things I wanted in a man had changed since meeting him. I never really thought about wanting to date a mama's boy until I met him (not that he would ever call himself that!) and realized that he knew how to treat women because he knew how to respect his mother. Likewise, I was also able to see where he fell short. I wanted someone who could make me laugh and though Adrian and I had a lot of fun, I never found myself belly-laughing in his presence. That didn't mean that we wouldn't have a great relationship, I just had to decide how big a priority that was for me, and if it was something I could do without. I didn't need to be consistently disappointed by it; I could just accept it and move on.

Date Like *This*: Learn to Trust

Remember Leslie, the fashion designer who sent the Jets text? Well, less than a year later, Leslie fell for Damon, a new client of mine and one heck of a catch. Damon was a handsome Wall Street trader and a part-time philanthropist. Hot, rich (though that shouldn't be your top priority), and he loved kids? Leslie fell hard and fast, and so did Damon. They seemed like a perfect match from the start. And this time Leslie stayed out of the texting trap and learned to hold the reins.

Whether you have had sex with him or not, you have been building intimacy since day one, getting to know and trust him step by step, week by week, date by date.

Except as time went on, it became clear that Leslie had no intention of letting go at all. She was such a type-A personality that she was afraid that if she lost any control, she would lose it all. Listen, I've never *not* been accused of being a type-A personality, so believe me, I get it. It's a fine balancing act, but as I explained to Leslie, we can work through it. We worked on her ability to trust what was happening between her and Damon. But before Leslie had come to me for help, Damon began to get nervous himself.

He would ask her why she wasn't opening up, and she would reply, "I'm just learning to trust you."

By their eighth week, Damon was wondering if Leslie was ever going to be able to let down her guard. He wrote:

From: Damon
Subject: Leslie

Hey Amy,
So I'm not quite sure what to do with the Leslie situation. As I had told you in the past it seems like she has real trouble talking to me. She said again that she's beginning to trust me, which makes me wonder when will she stop "beginning" and actually trust? I feel like she knows so much about me and I know 10 percent about her, unless that's all there is, in which case, that sucks. Not sure where to go from here. I like her so much and we have a great time, but I'm getting tired of pulling teeth.

D

If you feel like you are at the Week Two level of trust with someone when you're in Week Eight, then you need to look at where that's coming from. If it's from him, if you feel like something isn't right, then you need to decide if this is someone you're ever going to be able to trust. And if it's you, then you need to open up about why you're having that problem. If it's something from your past, explain that to him. Share why you need to take it slow, or why you are afraid. Trust is a bridge that is built one piece at a time. Even if you do it slowly, by giving him small pieces of information about why you feel that way, you will see why he is a man worth trusting. Leslie came to me before it became a real problem, and was able to go back to Damon with a more open heart, which is probably why they are still together to this day.

Not Like *That*: Obsession is a Nasty Perfume

Often we are not suspicious over nothing, and even more often, we are simply suspicious out of fear or leftover baggage from a prior relationship. If in your gut, you know something is up with your guy, acting crazy isn't going to make it better. If you can't trust him, whether it's his fault or yours, then you're not in the right relationship.

I know we have all been tempted to read text messages or have encountered an open e-mail account and couldn't help but see what was in the inbox. So don't worry, that doesn't mean you're nutso. Considering, or even accidentally looking at, one of these things, does not a stalker make. However, if these behaviors are executed with the sole aim to find some dish on your man, then you need to seriously ask yourself whether he is someone you should be with. And, perhaps more important, you need to seriously ask yourself whether you're ready to be in a relationship with anyone.

THE FAST TRACK TO CRAZY TOWN

I will tell you right now that once you walk into Crazy Town, it's really hard to get out. The minute you find yourself doing one of the following things, step back and ask what's prompting the behavior.

Here are eight warning signs that you are walking into bunny-boiling territory, a place that no self-respecting woman should ever go:

1. You are looking through his text messages.
2. You are searching his pockets for evidence of . . . something.
3. You have checked his e-mails or have logged into his FB account.
4. You have looked over his credit card bill or cell phone statement.
5. You are following him or trying to set a trap to catch him.
6. You have searched through his personal belongings.
7. You question any unidentified call or are suspicious of who he talks to.
8. You get upset if he does anything without you.

obsession *n.*: a persistent idea or desire that dominates your thoughts; the nasty offspring of distrust; the easiest way to kill a relationship.

Some of us might have some more work to do on ourselves before we can be in a partnership. Whether that means therapy, spirituality, or just taking some alone time to figure out what's going on in our heads, we need to decide whether a relationship might be too much. If you are engaging in unhealthy behaviors, you need to pull back and take a look at what you are doing and why. And then you need to put that nasty bottle of obsession away, and decide whether this is a relationship you should be in or are ready to be in.

Because the fact is, by this point, you have proven to each other that you're committed. You should have built a strong enough foundation by now that you can set any true and legitimate fears aside. So enjoy the relationship—don't obsess over it.

Date Like *This*: Keep the Pressure Off

In many ways, Week Eight is no different from Weeks One through Seven. Just like before, the minute you rush ahead and pretend you've been in this relationship for longer than you have, well, that's the minute you miss out on the relationship you're having. You are not in month six, or even month three, and you're definitely not in year two. No, you are right at the beginning. This is the place where the masks are beginning to fall away, where you are perhaps meeting each other's siblings or even parents, where you are now exclusively dating and neither of you is afraid to say it. Heck, maybe you have even changed your relationship status on Facebook. But you are still *getting to know each other.*

There are certain things that should be happening by now. He should have initiated the exclusivity conversation. If he hasn't then it is time for you to decide whether this is someone you want to continue dating. Tell him that you are looking for a relationship and if he isn't, then you're ready to move on. That doesn't mean you should ask him to be in a relationship, but he shouldn't bring up the topic in a last-ditch effort to keep you. If he goes out of his way to save the relationship, and demonstrates what he should have by now—that he is ready for a committed relationship with you—you may reconsider.

Otherwise, if you're dating exclusively, and particularly, if you are having sex, then there's no need to rush. Enjoy this stage. You've worked hard to get here so bask in what you've learned.

Last year, my friend Tasha was dating this great guy Samuel. Things were moving along at a steady pace, but once she felt they were exclusive, she thought that it was time to take things to the next level: Thanksgiving with her family. I'll admit, celebrating the holidays early on in a relationship is tricky, but here's the deal. If you weren't dating, you would both probably have holiday plans (it's not like Valentine's Day), so stick with those. If you stay together, there will always be another chance.

FUN FACT: A relationship is not an open wound. No need to apply pressure.

Unfortunately, Samuel agreed with me, and told Tasha he felt it was a little early for that. Tasha was hurt and a big fight ensued. It wasn't that Tasha was mad, but she felt rejected. And I think underneath that, she was embarrassed, because she knew she was applying unnecessary pressure that came back to bite her in the you-know-where.

Not Like *That*: Don't Start Hearing Wedding Bells

I know this is hard. We meet Mister Right and suddenly we want to skip everything in between and get to the big day. But relationships are a journey, and I can promise you, a wedding is far from a destination. It's one day among the many you two will hopefully share.

So why do you want to rush? These weeks, months, and maybe even years ahead are the most special time in your relationship. It's important to take time and let your relationship develop naturally.

How many whirlwind marriages do you know that have lasted? Not many. When a man and woman come together they need to build the life they are creating together slowly; not just slap some bricks and mortar together and call it a house.

Sadly, I see this happen way too often. Last year, I watched one of my clients singlehandedly destroy what could have been a great relationship because she got *way* too ahead of herself. Nancy is a hair stylist from Chicago who thought her dreams were coming true as soon as her man, Miguel, popped the question—no, not that question, the commitment one. Nancy immediately assumed her dating life was over and that they would be married within eighteen to twenty-four months and starting a family before she turned thirty.

Unfortunately for her, Miguel was looking at their relationship one day at a time. If something went wrong, he took it in stride, and figured it was something they would either grow from or they wouldn't. But for Nancy, every trouble in their relationship spelled D-I-V-O-R-C-E, even though they were still years away from being M-A-R-R-I-E-D. She just couldn't relax into what was happening in that moment because she was always so worried about how it was going to affect their future.

Dating someone who is always secretly freaking out about whether or not you are going to get married is not a lot of fun. When Nancy and Miguel had been together around six months, Miguel forgot to pay a parking ticket. The payment had doubled and the DMV sent him a letter. Now, what Nancy was doing reading his mail at six months is another story, but when Miguel got home, she lost it on him. She called him irresponsible, and told him she didn't know if she could trust someone who would do such a thing.

She told me later that he looked at her, and asked, "Forget to pay a parking ticket?"

She already had her reply waiting in her head: "Yes. I mean, how do you expect me to have children with you someday if you aren't responsible enough to mail in a check?" But she stopped herself and realized, "What the hell am I thinking?" They were in their mid-twenties. Miguel had never even brought up children and that was probably a good thing, but here she was acting like they were in their thirties with two kids and a mortgage when really they were just a young couple having fun. Sadly, she never had the chance to find out if she and Miguel would have made it to two kids and a mortgage. He broke up with her the next month, explaining that he didn't want to date someone who nagged him all the time. And Nancy had to take a long hard look at what her role had been in pushing the relationship to the brink.

Often, when women start hearing wedding bells, we start acting different. We start critiquing men based on roles we think they're going to play in the future: husband, father, in-law to our family, rather than on a relationship of eight weeks. We forget that for right now they are just our boyfriends. And that's a wonderful thing. Enjoy this stage!

Date Like *This*: Create a Partnership

The best situation is when two sincere people who share the same core values are ready to be in a relationship without sacrificing their own lives and interests. Neither of you should *need* the other person, but you should certainly love being with each other. It's called a balanced and healthy partnership.

Ultimatums or threats won't work. That's not a partnership; that's called fascism. And nobody likes a fascist.

Of course, as you continue along in this relationship, you should always continue to analyze and evaluate whether you are with the right person and if you are in the right partnership. There's no point in wasting either your time or his if it's time for the relationship to end. That's why I tell my clients that the evaluation period goes on forever. No matter whether you are in your eighth week, or eighth year, the key to a healthy relationship is that it needs frequent checkups. It's like going to the doctor: a lot of times illness hides undetected until we take the time to have an exam and see what needs to be fixed. Relationships are no different.

My client Tarina, the nutritionist who learned that dating

multiple people is important, finally found a long-term relationship, but after a couple of months, she began to worry that it was going stale. I reminded her about the feedback forms that most of my clients fill out after their dates (a version is included in the back of this book). I suggested that she start filling it out every time she and her man had a "date." At this point, a date is any previously scheduled time where the two of you go out alone, just as you did in the beginning. She wrote me the following week:

> *From: Tarina*
> *Subject: Rut*
>
> *I did what you told me, and then I waited. Two weeks went by and we hadn't gone on one "date." So sad to think that we started off with so much romance and were already fizzling out like old people. So I decided to start making more plans with friends. Last night, the ladies and I went to dinner and a movie. When I talked to Tom afterward, he replied, "God, we haven't been to the movies in a while." I kept my mouth shut but all I could think was "Bingo!"*

Partnership demands work. It's not like you end up with a boyfriend and, bam, you're done. No, being a part of a relationship means that you both need to assess where you are at and where it's going.

Continue to evaluate the situation and then change your behavior to show what you are looking for in a relationship. By simply making yourself busier, or refusing to settle for what your new boyfriend is offering, you can continue to keep the relationship exciting and both of you engaged. Your partner, if he is also behaving like a partner, will get the hint, and he will work to bring up his end of the deal. Remember, there are no ultimatums between partners. There are only clear communication and consistent action—two equals working together to make a special whole.

Not Like *That*: Don't Lose Your Balance

Okay, brace yourselves. I am going to tell you a very sad story about what can happen if you lose yourself and your identity to a relationship. Dating requires balance, and that means balance in your own life, too. As we've said before, there is nothing more pathetic than the girl who sacrifices her whole life in order to be some guy's girlfriend. It's not a grown-up thing to do, it's not attractive, and it's not a sustainable setup for the relationship.

Last year, one of my clients contacted me out of the blue. Sergio is a UN analyst and outrigger competitor. He had a busy and full life but when he came to me, he explained that one thing was missing: a woman to share it with. So after a number of dates, we found Sergio his woman—Elissa. Elissa is a neuroscientist with a Mother Teresa heart who walks into any room and turns heads. Disgusting, I know. After a month or so they started dating exclusively, and after about three months, I lost touch with them. And then Sergio e-mailed me this:

From: Sergio
Subject: Elissa

Hi Amy,
Sorry it's been a while. I know you reached out around the holidays, but things were a little crazy. Anyway, I just wanted to check in with you about Elissa. Everything was going fine and then one day last week, I was heading out to an outrigger competition with the guys and she was at my place. She's spent more and more time there over the last few months. I asked her what she was doing that day and she just shrugged. I suggested she see some of her friends and then I realized I hadn't seen any of her friends in a while. It just seems like all of my friends are now her friends. It hit me that she didn't actually have anything to do unless I was there—or she was at work or in the lab. I was like, shit, when did this happen? I got pretty annoyed but more than that I just felt kind of sad. How did she change so quickly? You got any insight?

Thanks,
Serg

You bet I have some insight! What the heck is Elissa doing? Never be left, or caught, sitting on the couch with nothing to do. I'm not saying never feel free to relax and watch television—we all deserve a day off. But never put yourself in the place where you don't actually have anything else to do, or anyone to do it with. Remember, life does not end when you get a boyfriend, and the best way to keep your relationship healthy is to stay healthy yourself. This means having your own life, your own friends, your own hobbies, and your own identity. Poor Sergio didn't know what to do with the wet rag sitting on his couch. And I don't blame him! We should never lose ourselves to a relationship. And the minute we do, we risk losing the relationship.

Date Like *This*: Enjoy, Enjoy, Enjoy—You Got This!

So, what next? Remember that this book is your friend. Whether you're in Week One, Week Seven, or in a happily committed relationship, use your trusted highlighter to pick up new thoughts and new behaviors that you might need to change.

You have made it through the first eight weeks, you have completed dating boot camp, and you are now armed with the skills and confidence to have a successful relationship. Does that mean that the boyfriend you have today will be your husband tomorrow? Who knows? But I do know that you can apply these tools over and over to help you navigate both your single and your relationship lives.

Because dating is never about the destination, it is always about the journey. So if you get to Week Two, and it doesn't pan out, start again. If you're in Week Four, and it falters, go back to Week One. If you get to year one and you break up, pick this book up and try again. Yes, you're bound to get a little scraped and bruised, but if you've ever been in love you know it's worth it. You are worth it.

Recently, I was on a first date with a friend of a friend. Nathan is a stockbroker who used to do stand-up comedy. He had me laughing the whole night. But I really got him when he asked what I did (as if he didn't know!), and I told him I was a matchmaker. He asked me, "How are you a dating expert and still single?"

I laughed—it's not the first time I've gotten that question—and replied, "Just because I'm an expert, doesn't mean I'm not human."

"All right, expert. How are we doing tonight?" he asked.

I thought about it. Do I answer him and be honest, telling him I am nervous or that I already really like him? No. Do I tell him that I Googled him and have already decided that we would look great in a church ceremony? No. Do I tell him that I have been waiting for a date like this for a while? No.

Instead, I just smiled, and said, "I'm having a good time. How about you?"

Because that is what dating should be: a good time. You should have fun—enjoy, enjoy, enjoy! You got this. You own this. You are seeing someone you like, you are sitting across the table and you are getting to know each other. You are in your second, third, fifth, eighth week of dating and you know that you have met someone special. And is that because you followed these guidelines? No. But what you did do is make sure you didn't sabotage a good thing out of fear or worry or naïveté. You relaxed and enjoyed it, held on to the reins, and respected yourself and your own power, and you are now ready for whatever comes next.

WEEK EIGHT: CHOOSE YOUR OWN RELATIONSHIP

Week Eight is far from the end; in fact, it's just the beginning. This is the week when you firmly set the foundation of the relationship to come. Never losing sight of whether or not the relationship is working, you should create a new routine and new rhythm with your new man. From sex to dating to spending time with friends, both of you are adapting to this wonderful thing in your lives. But as you fall more deeply, you need to make sure that you don't lose yourself to the relationship or to your own worries. Any sign of obsession or codependence should be met with major changes—even if that means taking some time off to restructure your own schedule and set new boundaries. There is no need to always have yet another "conversation." Sometimes just a couple of simple choices can set the two of you right back on track.

As you continue down the road to romance, remember to stay true to yourself, your friends, and your passions, retaining your identity even as you take on the role of "girlfriend." Love is not a destination; it is a journey. And it is one that needs to be kept healthy through consistent attention and evaluation. By keeping one eye on the fun and the other eye on how things are going, you'll be able to prevent major mishaps or breakdowns. And most important, when we create boundaries, outlining what kind of relationship we want, then we can finally relax, we can learn to trust, and we can enjoy, enjoy, enjoy! And finally, we can choose to be in the relationship we have always wanted.

Eight Steps to Everlasting

1. Hold on to the reins; though you might have given them some slack, remember to use your influence to control the pace of the relationship.
2. Stay calm and busy. Just because you have a boyfriend doesn't mean that's all you have. Don't turn your back on your interests and friends; they're more important than ever!
3. Do not start obsessing. If you start behaving crazy, see what is motivating you to act that way. Is it you or is it him?
4. Remember, you are still getting to know each other. So no invites to the holidays or dinner with your family. Take it slow.
5. You're not getting married . . . yet. So don't treat him like your husband—enjoy him as your boyfriend.
6. You are building a partnership so let your guard down, get to know each other more, and focus on building more intimacy.
7. Don't stop evaluating. Relationships demand hard work and consistent attention. Give your relationship a healthy checkup from time to time to make sure it's going in the right direction.
8. Have fun! Fall in love, enjoy each other, and remember, don't take yourself or the relationship too seriously. It has all just begun.

Feedback Form

Name of your date: ______________________________

Place you met and time/date: ______________________

____

Length of your date: ____________________________

How do you rate your date (on a scale of 1 to 10)?_______

Do you plan to see him again? ____________________

How did the date go? ___________________________

____

____

What was fun about it? __________________________

____

____

____

What could have been improved? ___________________

____

____

____